IOT ARMAGEDDON

Securing the Internet of Everything Against Invisible Attacks

Adedayo Jigida

Preface

This book began with a simple observation: we are surrounded by devices we no longer see. Phones, cars, homes, even our bodies each is connected, each is vulnerable. In writing this work, I sought to bring into focus the hidden risks we accept in exchange for convenience. The stories within are not distant futures; they are present realities unfolding across the globe. I approached the subject not with fear, but with urgency, and a belief that awareness is the first step toward action. *IoT Armageddon* is both a mirror and a warning, showing us what is at stake if we remain complacent. At the same time, it offers pathways toward resilience, because technology need not be our undoing. My hope is that every reader will leave with eyes open and resolve strengthened. Together, we can build a secure foundation for the connected world ahead.

Introduction

The world is standing on the edge of a digital revolution where the physical and virtual realms are no longer separated but woven together in ways humanity has never experienced before. This new paradigm is powered by the Internet of Things, a vast, interconnected ecosystem of smart devices, sensors, and networks that extend far beyond computers and smartphones. IoT is already embedded in our homes, workplaces, transportation systems, supply chains, healthcare, and even the infrastructure that sustains modern life. From thermostats that automatically adjust to our comfort, to cars that drive themselves, to medical implants that transmit vital health data in real time, IoT has transformed convenience into a way of life and data into the new currency of society. Yet, with this extraordinary innovation comes an equally extraordinary risk. As we rush headlong into the age of hyperconnectivity, we are also constructing a digital battlefield where unseen adversaries exploit unseen vulnerabilities. Each "thing" on the Internet of Things represents not only a point of innovation, but also a potential point of intrusion. The same interconnectedness that enables efficiency and intelligence can, if compromised, magnify harm on a scale previously unimaginable.

This book, IoT Armageddon: Securing the Internet of Everything Against Invisible Attacks, is both a warning and a guide. It is a warning that the conveniences of IoT come with hidden costs, costs that may not become apparent until they erupt in catastrophic ways. It is also a guide, offering a roadmap to understanding the threats, technologies, and strategies necessary to defend against the looming security crisis in our hyperconnected world. The Internet of Everything does not stop at linking devices; it extends to connecting people, data, and processes in a complex web of digital intelligence. A refrigerator can talk to a grocery store, a fitness tracker can share health data with a hospital, and a traffic sensor can communicate with an entire city's power grid. Analysts predict that tens of billions of connected devices will populate the globe within this decade, creating a world where virtually every object is capable of sensing, communicating, and acting. This exponential growth offers profound opportunities. Businesses can optimize operations with predictive analytics. Cities can become "smart," reducing traffic congestion and pollution. Farmers can harness sensors for precision agriculture, maximizing yields while conserving resources. Healthcare systems can monitor patients remotely, bringing care to rural or underserved areas.

But this massive interconnectedness is also a digital powder keg. Each device is a potential gateway for malicious actors. Each dataset is a potential target. Each interdependency, where one system relies on another, creates a domino effect, where a single breach can ripple across industries, communities, and even nations. Unlike traditional warfare, IoT attacks are often invisible. They may not announce themselves with explosions or alarms, but their consequences can be just as devastating. A hacked pacemaker can threaten a patient's life, a hijacked fleet of delivery drones can paralyze a city, and ransomware unleashed on a smart grid can plunge millions into darkness. The enemy in the IoT era does not need bombs or armies, it needs only code, persistence, and an understanding of hidden vulnerabilities.

The most frightening aspect of IoT threats is their stealth. A compromised device may silently gather data for months or years before anyone detects it. Malware can spread across thousands of devices, forming botnets capable of overwhelming global networks. Hackers can manipulate sensor data, causing systems to make dangerous decisions based on false inputs. An autonomous vehicle might be guided off course by corrupted GPS signals, or a water treatment facility could release harmful chemicals because its sensors were tampered with. These invisible attacks exploit not only technical weaknesses, but also human complacency. Most consumers assume their smart devices are secure and rarely question the invisible pathways their data travels. Organizations often prioritize cost and convenience over security, deploying devices with default passwords, outdated software, or no mechanism for updates. Governments struggle to regulate a landscape where the pace of innovation far outstrips the creation of protective frameworks.

The term "Armageddon" is not chosen lightly. While it evokes images of apocalypse, it is an apt metaphor for the potential collapse that could result from large-scale IoT insecurity. Imagine a coordinated cyber-assault in which millions of everyday devices, washing machines, cameras, vehicles, even medical implants, are weaponized simultaneously. The result could be widespread outages, economic paralysis, and loss of life. We have already seen glimpses of this future. In 2016, the Mirai botnet harnessed insecure IoT devices to unleash one of the largest distributed denial-of-service attacks in history, temporarily taking down major websites and services. That attack, as disruptive as it was, represented only a fraction of what is possible. Future threats will not merely interrupt access to the internet; they will disrupt the very systems upon which human lives and national security depend.

The looming crisis is not inevitable, but it is plausible. The interconnectedness of the Internet of Everything means vulnerabilities are no longer isolated; they are systemic. A single weak link can compromise an entire chain of devices and networks. In a hyperconnected world, local failures can quickly escalate into global catastrophes. That is why this book calls for action. Securing the IoT requires not only technological solutions but also cultural, organizational, and political transformations. Security must shift from being an afterthought to being the foundation of design. Every device, every protocol, every line of code must be scrutinized through the lens of security from the very beginning.

Throughout this book, we will examine strategies for defending against invisible attacks. These include zero-trust architectures that assume no device or user is inherently trustworthy, artificial intelligence systems capable of detecting anomalies across complex networks, encryption techniques that safeguard communication among devices, robust firmware and patch management to prevent outdated vulnerabilities, blockchain systems for authenticating IoT data, and global standards that enforce security baselines across industries. Yet security is not only about technology; it is also about people and processes. Consumers must become more aware of the risks they take when adopting IoT. Organizations must allocate resources to protecting their networks instead of treating security as a compliance checkbox. Governments must work together to create international frameworks that address threats without borders. And innovators must design with foresight, anticipating not only how devices will be used but also how they could be abused.

The stakes of IoT insecurity extend far beyond financial loss or technical disruption. Our health, privacy, freedoms, and even survival may hinge on how we address the challenges of securing the Internet of Everything. The future we face is not prewritten. We can either allow a digital Wild West to dictate our reality, or we can build resilient, secure systems capable of withstanding invisible attacks. This book does not seek to instill fear but to inspire action. Fear alone paralyzes, while knowledge empowers. By understanding the risks, recognizing the stakes, and implementing effective strategies, we can prevent the nightmare of an IoT Armageddon and instead harness the transformative potential of this technology safely and responsibly.

The Internet of Everything is inevitable. Whether it becomes a world of innovation and efficiency or one of insecurity and chaos depends on the choices we make today. The future is being written not just in lines of code, but in the collective resolve of people, organizations, and governments to safeguard what they are building. The battle for IoT security is not on the horizon, it is already here. Awareness is our first weapon, strategy our second, and decisive action our third. IoT Armageddon is more than a book about technology; it is a survival guide for the digital age.

Chapter One

Dawn of the Internet of Everything

The journey of the Internet of Things (IoT) began innocently enough with simple devices like fitness trackers, connected thermostats, and smart lighting. Each new gadget promised convenience, efficiency, and seamless integration into our daily lives. In the early 2010s, these devices operated largely in isolation, providing basic functionality that seemed almost quaint by today's standards. A fitness tracker counted steps, a smart thermostat learned heating preferences, and connected light bulbs could be dimmed from a smartphone app. These were incremental improvements to existing products rather than revolutionary changes to how we lived.

Over time, however, these innovations transformed into sophisticated ecosystems, where multiple devices interact with each other, share data continuously, and communicate with cloud-based artificial intelligence systems that analyze patterns and make predictions. What emerged is now called the Internet of Everything a vast, interconnected network that extends far beyond individual gadgets to encompass entire environments, infrastructures, and ways of life. Suddenly, refrigerators could not only monitor their contents but also place grocery orders based on consumption patterns and dietary preferences stored in the cloud. Doorbells evolved into comprehensive security systems that could scan faces, recognize family members versus strangers, and coordinate with indoor cameras and smart locks to create seamless entry experiences. Watches became sophisticated health monitoring stations that could detect irregular heart rhythms, predict potential cardiac events, and automatically contact emergency services while sharing real-time health data with physicians.

The transformation accelerated as artificial intelligence and machine learning capabilities became embedded within these ecosystems. Devices began to learn from user behavior, anticipate needs, and make autonomous decisions. Smart homes evolved to understand daily routines automatically adjusting temperature before residents woke up, brewing coffee when morning alarms sounded, and dimming lights as bedtime approached. The concept of manual control became increasingly obsolete as predictive automation took over.

But this evolution wasn't just about personal convenience or incremental improvements to domestic life. On a larger scale, entire smart cities emerged, powered by vast networks of connected sensors, cameras, and monitoring systems that control traffic flow in real-time, monitor air quality across different neighborhoods, optimize energy grids based on consumption patterns, and coordinate emergency response systems. Cities like Barcelona, Singapore, and Amsterdam became living laboratories where IoT technology was integrated into every aspect of urban planning and management. Traffic lights could communicate with approaching vehicles to optimize flow, parking meters could guide drivers to available spaces, and waste management systems could signal when bins needed emptying.

In industries across the spectrum, IoT became the backbone of what experts call Industry 4.0 a new era of manufacturing and business operations built on automation, predictive maintenance, and comprehensive logistics tracking. Factory floors transformed into networks of connected machines that could predict failures before they occurred, automatically order replacement parts, and optimize production schedules based on real-time demand data. Supply chains became transparent from raw materials to final delivery, with every package, container, and vehicle tracked continuously across global networks.

The agricultural sector experienced perhaps one of the most dramatic transformations through precision farming techniques enabled by IoT. Sensors embedded in soil could monitor moisture levels, nutrient content, and pH balance, automatically triggering irrigation systems and fertilizer applications. Drones equipped with cameras and sensors could survey vast crop fields, identifying areas of stress or disease that required attention. Livestock wore connected devices that monitored health, location, and behavior patterns, enabling farmers to manage herds with unprecedented precision.

The line between the digital and physical world began to blur as these systems became more sophisticated and interconnected. What started as discrete applications evolved into comprehensive digital twins' virtual representations of physical systems that could simulate, predict, and optimize real-world operations. This interconnected reality was no longer just a convenience or luxury it became fundamental to how modern society functions, creating dependencies that extend into every aspect of human civilization.

How Connectivity Redefined Human Life

Connectivity has redefined not just how humans interact with technology, but fundamentally transformed how societies function, how relationships are maintained, and how basic human needs are met. The smartphone became far more than a communication device it evolved into the central command center for human existence, giving individuals unprecedented control over homes, cars, workplaces, and social interactions with a single tap or voice command. This pocket-sized computer became the primary interface through which people navigate their daily lives, from waking up to alarm clocks that gradually increase light intensity to mimic natural sunrise, to falling asleep to sounds controlled by apps that monitor sleep patterns and optimize rest cycles.

The transformation of healthcare represents one of the most significant shifts enabled by IoT connectivity. Traditional healthcare, which relied on periodic visits to medical facilities and reactive treatment of symptoms, evolved into a continuous monitoring and predictive wellness system. Patients with chronic conditions like diabetes could have their blood sugar levels monitored continuously by sensors that communicate directly with healthcare providers, triggering interventions before dangerous spikes or drops occur. Elderly individuals living independently could wear devices that detect falls, monitor vital signs, and assess cognitive function, enabling them to remain in their homes longer while providing family members and caregivers with peace of mind.

Remote patient monitoring expanded beyond simple vital sign tracking to include sophisticated analysis of movement patterns, speech patterns, medication adherence, and even subtle changes in daily routines that might indicate emerging health issues. Doctors could observe patients from miles away using connected medical devices, accessing more comprehensive and continuous data than was ever possible through traditional office visits. This shift enabled preventive medicine on an unprecedented scale, with AI systems analyzing vast amounts of health data to identify risk factors and suggest interventions before symptoms appeared.

Education, too, embraced IoT through virtual classrooms that connected students and teachers across geographical boundaries, interactive whiteboards that responded to touch and gesture commands, and personalized learning tools that adapted in real-time to student performance and learning styles. Educational environments became responsive and dynamic, with sensors monitoring engagement levels, identifying when students were struggling with concepts, and automatically adjusting content difficulty and presentation methods. This created truly personalized learning experiences where no two students received identical instruction.

The workplace underwent equally dramatic changes as IoT enabled new forms of collaboration, productivity measurement, and environmental optimization. Office buildings became intelligent environments that could track occupancy patterns, optimize lighting and temperature for productivity, and even monitor air quality to ensure optimal cognitive performance. Remote work capabilities expanded beyond simple video conferencing to include shared virtual workspaces where teams could collaborate on projects as if they were physically present together.

Yet, the most profound transformation lies in the fundamental shift of human expectations and behavior patterns. People now assume that every process, whether it's ordering food, commuting, managing finances, or maintaining social relationships, should be instantaneous, optimized, and require minimal conscious effort. The concept of waiting, which was once an accepted part of life, became increasingly intolerable. Traffic delays triggered automatic rerouting through navigation apps, restaurant reservations were made instantly through voice commands, and entertainment was available on-demand across multiple platforms simultaneously.

Connectivity changed the rhythm of human life, moving society away from scheduled, predictable patterns toward an "always on" mindset where immediate response and constant availability became the norm. Social interactions shifted from planned meetings and phone calls to continuous streams of messages, updates, and notifications that created an expectation of immediate response. The boundary between work and personal time dissolved as connected devices made it possible to be productive from anywhere at any time.

This transformation extended beyond individual behavior to reshape entire social structures. Communities formed around shared interests and experiences that transcended geographical boundaries, enabled by IoT platforms that connected like-minded individuals globally. Local businesses could reach global markets through connected platforms, while global corporations could provide personalized, local experiences through data collected by IoT devices.

In this hyperconnected world, to be offline became more than just an inconvenience, it represented a form of social and economic isolation that could impact career prospects, social relationships, and access to basic services. Digital literacy and connected device ownership became prerequisites for full participation in modern society, creating new forms of inequality between those with access to advanced connectivity and those without.

The Fragile Web Beneath Our Comfort

What most fail to recognize, however, is that this interconnected ecosystem, despite its appearance of sophistication and reliability, is held together by surprisingly fragile threads of technology that are often insecure by design and vulnerable to catastrophic failure. The rush to bring IoT products to market consistently prioritized functionality and cost reduction over security and resilience, creating a vast attack surface that grows larger and more vulnerable with each new connected device that comes online.

Many IoT devices are manufactured as cheaply as possible, with minimal regard for cybersecurity principles that have been established for decades in traditional computing. These devices often use outdated processors, run simplified operating systems with known vulnerabilities, and include minimal security features to keep production costs low and maximize profit margins. The pressure to deliver products quickly in competitive markets means that security testing is often superficial or skipped entirely, with manufacturers assuming that basic encryption and authentication will be sufficient protection.

The scale of this problem is staggering. Billions of these devices are shipped to consumers and businesses worldwide each year, creating an enormous network of potential entry points for malicious actors. Default passwords remain unchanged on millions of devices because users are either unaware of the security implications or find the process of changing credentials too complex or time-consuming. Even when users do attempt to secure their devices, many IoT products lack user-friendly interfaces for security configuration, making proper security setup difficult or impossible for average consumers.

Software maintenance represents another critical vulnerability in the IoT ecosystem. Unlike traditional computers and smartphones, which receive regular security updates through established channels, many IoT devices are abandoned by their manufacturers shortly after sale. Companies may go out of business, discontinue product lines, or simply decide that providing ongoing security updates is not profitable. This leaves devices with outdated software that contains known security flaws, lingering unpatched on networks for years or even decades.

The interconnected nature of IoT networks means that these vulnerabilities cascade and amplify across entire systems. A single compromised device can become a foothold for attackers to move laterally through networks, accessing increasingly sensitive systems and data. Home networks that were once relatively isolated become bridges between personal devices and corporate systems as remote work becomes more prevalent. Industrial IoT systems that control critical infrastructure can be accessed through seemingly innocuous consumer devices that share network connections.

Network infrastructure itself presents additional vulnerabilities as it strains to handle the massive volume of data generated by billions of connected devices. Many networks were designed for human-generated traffic patterns and struggle to cope with the constant streams of sensor data, telemetry, and automated communications that characterize IoT environments. This can lead to network congestion, service degradation, and additional attack vectors as network administrators implement quick fixes that prioritize functionality over security.

The paradox becomes increasingly stark as our analysis deepens: while IoT has become the foundation of modern comfort, convenience, and productivity, it simultaneously represents our greatest collective vulnerability. Every connected device that makes life easier also creates a potential pathway for disruption, surveillance, or attack. Every system that becomes more automated and efficient also becomes more dependent on vulnerable technologies that most users do not understand and cannot secure effectively.

Our societal dependence on IoT connectivity has outpaced our ability to secure it by several decades. The security expertise, infrastructure, and practices needed to protect these systems safely exist but have not been implemented at the scale and speed required to match IoT deployment. This creates a dangerous gap where billions of devices operate with inadequate protection, and millions of users depend on systems they cannot secure themselves. The economic incentives driving IoT development actively work against security improvements. Manufacturers compete on features, price, and time-to-market rather than security quality. Consumers generally cannot evaluate the security characteristics of IoT products and make purchasing decisions based on convenience and cost rather than protection. The true costs of poor IoT security in terms of privacy violations, system disruptions, and potential catastrophic failures are externalized to society rather than borne by manufacturers or users.

As the world marches deeper into the Internet of Everything, this fundamental fragility becomes not just a technical problem requiring technical solutions, but a comprehensive societal challenge that demands new approaches to technology governance, user education, and systems design. The comfortable, connected world that IoT has created rests on foundations that are far less stable than most people realize. This sets the stage for an inevitable confrontation between the convenience we have grown to depend upon and the catastrophic potential that lurks within the systems that provide it. The question is no longer whether these vulnerabilities will be exploited on a massive scale, but when, how extensively, and whether our society will be prepared to respond effectively when the fragile web beneath our comfort finally breaks under pressure.

Chapter Two

The Rise of Invisible Threats

The most unsettling aspect of cyber threats on the Internet of Things (IoT) era is not their sophistication, but their invisibility. Unlike traditional dangers where an intruder could be seen, heard, or confronted, digital threats often lurk unseen, woven into lines of code, patiently waiting for the right opportunity. For the average consumer, a hacked device doesn't burst into flames or display obvious warning signs. Instead, it continues to function normally, delivering the services it was designed for streaming movies, adjusting thermostats, or monitoring heart rates while secretly betraying its owner in ways that may never be discovered.

Malware designed for IoT devices rarely draws attention to itself. In fact, its effectiveness depends on the ability to remain hidden. A compromised security camera, for example, may still record footage as expected, even while secretly transmitting video streams to an unknown attacker halfway around the world. Routers infected with malicious software may continue to provide Wi-Fi access, but in the background, they are rerouting traffic, capturing sensitive data, or acting as nodes in a criminal network.

Unlike traditional computers, IoT devices have limited interfaces. A laptop or smartphone may reveal infection through pop-up ads, crashes, or sluggish performance, but a smart light bulb has no way to signal distress. A connected pacemaker, designed to regulate heartbeats, cannot display a flashing warning message when it is compromised. In this world of limited interfaces, invisibility is not just an advantage for attackers, it is almost guaranteed. The more deeply these devices embed themselves in our lives, the harder it becomes to detect when they turn against us.

Silent Infiltration: How Attacks Go Unnoticed

The stealth of IoT infiltration is not coincidental, it is a deliberate strategy. Hackers know that most IoT devices are deployed in a "set it and forget it" manner. Once installed, they are rarely updated, monitored, or even thought about again. This complacency creates the perfect breeding ground for long-term compromise.

The Mirai botnet, discovered in 2016, remains one of the most infamous examples. By exploiting weak default passwords in routers, cameras, and DVRs, Mirai enslaved hundreds of thousands of devices without their owners realizing. These devices carried on with their everyday tasks while secretly forming part of one of the most powerful botnets in history. When activated, this hidden army unleashed a record-breaking distributed denial-of-service (DDoS) attack on Dyn, a major Domain Name System (DNS) provider. Suddenly, websites like Twitter, Netflix, and Amazon became inaccessible to millions of users. The devices' owners never suspected their household gadgets were being used to help take down the internet.

The danger of silent infiltration extends beyond consumer electronics. In healthcare, infusion pumps, CT scanners, and wireless patient monitors have all been demonstrated to be vulnerable. A hacker could tamper with the dosage levels of life-sustaining drugs or alter imaging results without immediate detection. In factories, compromised sensors feeding inaccurate data into control systems could degrade product quality or disrupt operations for months before the anomalies were traced back to an attack. The silent nature of these intrusions is their deadliest characteristic: the ability to operate in the shadows long enough to cause deep, systemic harm.

Even governments are not immune. Intelligence agencies have reported cases where adversarial nations quietly infiltrated smart infrastructure. Unlike traditional acts of espionage, which may involve stolen documents or intercepted communications, IoT infiltrations provide persistent access to physical systems: power grids, traffic signals, and surveillance cameras. In such cases, the infiltration is often discovered not by the victim, but by chance through a suspicious network trace, a whistleblower, or sheer luck.

When Ordinary Devices Become Weapons

Perhaps the most alarming aspect of invisible threats is their ability to weaponize the ordinary. A child's internet-connected toy, a household refrigerator, or a smart TV might seem harmless. Yet, in the wrong hands, each of these devices can become a cog in a much larger machine of destruction.

The 2016 Dyn attack was only the beginning. Researchers have demonstrated the potential for IoT devices to be manipulated on a massive scale. In 2015, security researchers Charlie Miller and Chris Valasek famously hacked into a Jeep Cherokee over the internet, remotely controlling its steering, brakes, and transmission. The demonstration forced Fiat Chrysler to recall 1.4 million vehicles, a powerful reminder that even automobiles had become vulnerable to invisible attacks.

Consider, too, the Stuxnet worm, a sophisticated cyberweapon discovered in 2010. Though technically not an IoT attack in the consumer sense, Stuxnet targeted industrial control systems, specifically Iran's nuclear centrifuges. The worm was designed to silently manipulate the centrifuges' operation while feeding normal data back to monitoring systems, ensuring the sabotage went undetected for years. It was a chilling preview of how invisible attacks on connected devices could cause physical destruction while avoiding immediate detection.

Weaponization doesn't always take the form of catastrophic failure. Often, it involves subtle manipulations that destabilize trust. A hacked baby monitor that broadcasts a stranger's voice into a nursery may not crash the internet, but it can terrify families. A tampered smart meter could inflate electricity bills, eroding trust in utilities. These small-scale violations, replicated across millions of devices, represent another form of weaponization: the undermining of societal confidence in technology itself.

The Psychology of Invisible Threats

Beyond technical damage, invisible attacks carry profound psychological weight. Fear thrives on uncertainty, and what could be more uncertain than the suspicion that every device around you might be compromised? A laptop with a known virus can be wiped clean and restored, but how does one "clean" a refrigerator, thermostat, or implanted pacemaker? The idea that invisible enemies might be hiding in familiar objects generates a lingering sense of paranoia.

This erosion of trust has wider consequences. If consumers lose confidence in connected technologies, the very industries driving the IoT revolution could suffer. Smart cities, reliant on sensors for traffic control and energy efficiency, cannot function if citizens suspect that those sensors are unreliable or manipulated. Healthcare innovations, like remote patient monitoring, lose value if patients fear that hackers might alter their medical data. The invisible nature of these threats does not just endanger systems it endangers the social contract between people and technology.

Invisible attacks also create psychological asymmetry between attacker and victim. Hackers operate with confidence, knowing their work will likely go unnoticed. Victims, on the other hand, may never realize they were compromised. This imbalance creates a fertile environment for exploitation: a world where attackers feel empowered and defenders are perpetually on the back foot.

Future Scenarios: An Expanding Shadow

If the present is unsettling, the future may be even more so. As artificial intelligence merges with IoT, invisible threats will take on new dimensions. AI-driven malware could autonomously adapt to detection attempts, hiding deeper within systems and even creating decoys to mislead investigators. Such malware would not need human operators constantly directing it; it would learn, evolve, and persist on its own.

Quantum computing adds another layer of uncertainty. Today's encryption methods, while imperfect, still provide a degree of protection. But quantum-powered decryption could render current security protocols obsolete almost overnight.

If quantum capabilities fall into the hands of attackers, the invisible infiltrations of today could become unstoppable sieges tomorrow.

Another looming threat is the integration of IoT with critical infrastructure. Smart grids, autonomous vehicles, and connected military hardware are becoming realities. The compromise of a single IoT node in such environments could cascade into catastrophic consequences. Imagine a coordinated attack where traffic lights across a city are simultaneously hijacked, or a swarm of compromised delivery drones is repurposed into a weaponized fleet. These scenarios may sound like dystopian fiction, yet cybersecurity experts warn they are plausible extensions of today's vulnerabilities.

The rise of invisible threats in the Internet of Things era marks a profound shift in the nature of security. For centuries, humanity has understood threats as something tangible, observable, and immediate. But the threats now woven into our devices operate in silence, undetected until their consequences spill into the physical world. This silent war is already underway, fought not with bullets or bombs, but with code and compromised machines hidden in plain sight.

The paradox is stark: the devices that bring unprecedented convenience and efficiency also create unprecedented vulnerability. The very fabric of modern life, our homes, workplaces, hospitals, and cities is increasingly dependent on systems that may already be infiltrated. To survive this new era, societies must confront not only the technical challenges of securing IoT, but also the psychological and cultural implications of living with invisible, omnipresent threats.

The question is no longer whether these attacks will happen. They already are. The question is whether we will recognize them in time or whether the greatest dangers of the Internet of Everything will remain unseen until it is too late.

Chapter Three

Anatomy of an IoT Catastrophe

Every security system is only as strong as its weakest link, and on the Internet of Things (IoT), the weak links are everywhere. Unlike traditional networks, which may involve hundreds or thousands of nodes, IoT ecosystems can include millions, even billions, of devices, each one a potential point of failure. From smart refrigerators to connected heart monitors, each device is a doorway, and many of those doorways are left unlocked.

The problem begins with design philosophy. Many IoT devices are created with one goal in mind: functionality. Manufacturers rush products to market to capture growing demand, often neglecting security in the process. Default passwords remain unchanged, outdated firmware goes unpatched, and data streams remain unencrypted. Inexpensive devices are especially vulnerable; a smart light bulb purchased for a few dollars may have little or no built-in security, but once connected to a network, it can serve as a steppingstone for attackers.

The economics of IoT manufacturing exacerbate these vulnerabilities. Consumer electronics operate on razor-thin margins, where every penny counts in the battle for market share. Adding robust security features like encryption chips, secure boot mechanisms, and tamper-resistant hardware increases manufacturing costs that companies are reluctant to absorb. The result is a race to the bottom, where security becomes a luxury feature rather than a fundamental requirement. Consumers, focused on price and convenience, unknowingly purchase devices that transform their homes into potential battlegrounds.

The supply chain further complicates matters. IoT devices are rarely built entirely by a single company. Components come from multiple manufacturers across different countries, often with little oversight. A vulnerability in a microchip, a backdoor in firmware, or a poorly secured update mechanism can slip into millions of products distributed worldwide. Attackers know this. and they exploit it ruthlessly. For them, the challenge is not breaking through a fortified castle wall but finding the one open window among thousands.

Consider the complexity of a modern smart television. Its main processor might be manufactured in Taiwan, its wireless chip in South Korea, its camera module in China, and its firmware developed by contractors in Eastern Europe.

Each component represents a different security posture, a different set of standards, and a different potential vulnerability. When assembled, these components create a device where the security is only as strong as the weakest contributor in this global supply chain.

This reality makes IoT a hacker's paradise. A criminal doesn't need to compromise a fortified data center directly; instead, they can exploit the weakest link in the chain, perhaps a poorly secured webcam or a connected fish tank thermostat in a corporate lobby and then pivot from there into more sensitive systems. Once inside, attackers can escalate privileges, move laterally through networks, and ultimately gain access to systems that were assumed to be secure. This chain-reaction exploitation is the anatomy of catastrophe.

The situation is further complicated by the longevity mismatch between IoT devices and cybersecurity needs. While a smartphone might be replaced every two to three years, IoT devices are often expected to operate for a decade or more. A smart thermostat installed today might still be controlling a home's climate in 2035, long after its manufacturer has stopped providing security updates. This creates a growing population of zombie devices, technically functional but increasingly vulnerable as new attack vectors emerge and old protections become obsolete.

The Domino Effect of Compromise

IoT catastrophes rarely begin with a dramatic explosion. Instead, they unfold quietly, with one small breach cascading into larger failures, much like a row of dominoes falling in sequence. What begins as a single compromised device can spiral into a systemic collapse affecting millions of people.

Take the example of healthcare. A compromised connected infusion pump may initially seem like a contained problem. But that pump connects to a hospital's network, which also manages electronic health records, imaging systems, and critical monitoring devices. From there, attackers could exfiltrate patient data, alter diagnostic results, or even manipulate life-sustaining machines. The catastrophic potential is not just data loss, but human lives put at risk.

The healthcare scenario becomes even more frightening when considering the interconnected nature of modern medical facilities. A single hospital doesn't operate in isolation, it's part of a network that includes other hospitals, clinics, insurance companies, and pharmaceutical suppliers. A breach that begins with a compromised glucose monitor in one facility could potentially spread across an entire healthcare system, affecting thousands of patients and providers. The medical industry's increasing reliance on remote monitoring and telemedicine only expands the potential attack surface.

Transportation offers another chilling scenario. The Jeep Cherokee hack of 2015 demonstrated how attackers could remotely control a vehicle's steering and brakes through its infotainment system. Now imagine that same vulnerability weaponized across thousands of cars simultaneously. A coordinated attack could disable entire fleets, paralyze traffic in major cities, or create mass accidents on highways. The catastrophe would not be limited to individual drivers but would ripple outward, overwhelming emergency services and disrupting economies.

The transportation domino effect extends beyond individual vehicles to entire logistics networks. Modern shipping relies heavily on IoT sensors to track cargo, monitor vehicle health, and optimize routes. A coordinated attack on these systems could disrupt global supply chains, affecting everything from food distribution to medical supplies. The just-in-time delivery systems that make modern commerce efficient become fragility points when compromised, potentially causing shortages of essential goods within days.

Critical infrastructure presents perhaps the most frightening domino effect. Power grids, for example, are increasingly reliant on IoT sensors to balance supply and demand. If attackers compromise even a small subset of those sensors, they could feed false data into control systems, leading to blackouts across entire regions. In 2015, Ukraine experienced just such an event when hackers gained access to its power grid, plunging hundreds of thousands of people into darkness. While not solely an IoT attack, it underscored how interconnected systems can unravel under targeted infiltration.

The power grid example illustrates a critical vulnerability in modern infrastructure: the dependency cascade. When electrical power fails, it doesn't just leave buildings dark. Water treatment plants shut down, telecommunications networks fail, financial systems go offline, and transportation systems grind to a halt. A successful attack on IoT devices controlling one utility can rapidly cascade across multiple critical sectors, creating a systemic failure that affects every aspect of modern life.

Financial systems are similarly exposed. Banks and stock exchanges increasingly rely on IoT for surveillance, environmental monitoring, and logistics. A single compromised sensor could give attackers a foothold to disrupt trading platforms or manipulate data flows. In the age of digital finance, a few minutes of chaos could wipe out billions in value. The dominoes fall quickly when the stakes are global. Smart cities represent perhaps the ultimate domino scenario. As urban areas become more connected with smart traffic lights, environmental sensors, emergency response systems, and public Wi-Fi networks they create massive attack surfaces. A coordinated assault on a smart city's IoT infrastructure could simultaneously disrupt traffic, disable emergency services, manipulate environmental controls, and compromise public safety systems. The result would be urban chaos on a scale previously unimaginable.

Lessons from Real-World IoT Breaches

Real-world incidents provide sobering lessons about the anatomy of IoT catastrophes. The Mirai botnet remains one of the most notorious examples. By exploiting weak default passwords in everyday devices, Mirai created an army of zombie machines that launched devastating distributed denial-of-service (DDoS) attacks. The 2016 attack on Dyn crippled major internet platforms for hours, demonstrating how millions of seemingly insignificant devices could be marshaled into a weapon of mass disruption. The lesson was clear: even low-powered devices, when aggregated, become a formidable force.

The Mirai incident revealed the scale of IoT vulnerability in stark terms. The botnet eventually grew to include over 600,000 compromised devices, ranging from security cameras to home routers. What made Mirai particularly effective was its targeting strategy it didn't need sophisticated exploits, just the patience to scan the internet for devices using default credentials. The attack demonstrated that cybersecurity's weakest link isn't always technical sophistication but basic security hygiene.

The Stuxnet worm offers another critical lesson, though it targeted industrial control systems rather than consumer IoT. By subtly manipulating Iran's nuclear centrifuges while feeding false data to monitoring systems, Stuxnet remained undetected for years. It was the first known cyberweapon to cause physical destruction. The lesson here is chilling: invisible infiltrations can lead to catastrophic physical consequences, not just digital disruption. As IoT expands deeper into critical infrastructure, the potential for Stuxnet-like attacks multiplies exponentially.

Stuxnet's sophistication lay not just in its technical capabilities but in its understanding of the target environment. The malware was specifically designed to recognize and attack particular models of centrifuges, demonstrating that future IoT attacks might be equally targeted and devastating. The incident showed that state-level actors are willing and able to develop cyber weapons that cross the digital-physical boundary, raising the stakes for IoT security across all sectors. Medical devices have also revealed vulnerabilities with catastrophic implications. In 2017, the U.S. Food and Drug Administration (FDA) recalled nearly half a million pacemakers due to cybersecurity flaws that could allow hackers to alter pacing commands or drain batteries remotely. While no mass attack occurred, the potential was staggering: a vulnerability in devices keeping human hearts beating. The lesson is one of proximity. IoT doesn't just connect us digitally; it connects directly to our bodies, raising the stakes from financial or infrastructural damage to literal life and death.

The pacemaker incident highlighted a particularly troubling aspect of medical IoT: the impossible choice between connectivity and security. These devices need to communicate with monitoring systems and receive updates, but every connection creates potential vulnerabilities. Unlike a compromised smartphone that might leak personal data, a compromised medical device could literally kill its user. The medical device industry now faces the challenge of balancing life-saving connectivity with life-threatening security risks.

Even seemingly trivial devices have proven to be catastrophic gateways. In 2018, a casino in North America was hacked through an internet-connected fish tank thermometer. Attackers exploited the weakly secured device to pivot into the casino's network, stealing valuable data. Though this breach was not a life-threatening catastrophe, it highlighted a critical truth: attackers don't need to storm the front gates when a poorly secured side entrance is left wide open.

The fish tank incident became emblematic of IoT security's fundamental challenge: the expansion of the attack surface to include devices that were never designed with security in mind. The thermometer had no inherent reason to be connected to the internet beyond convenience, yet that connection created an entry point into a network containing millions of dollars in sensitive data. The incident demonstrated that in IoT ecosystems, every connected device no matter how seemingly innocent must be considered a potential security risk.

More recently, the 2021 attack on a Florida water treatment plant revealed another dimension of IoT vulnerability. Attackers gained access to the plant's control systems and briefly increased sodium hydroxide levels to dangerous concentrations before being detected. While this particular incident was caught quickly, it demonstrated how IoT devices controlling essential services can be weaponized to directly threaten public health. Each of these incidents teaches us the same underlying lesson: IoT catastrophes rarely look like the work of Hollywood villains. They are quiet, incremental, and opportunistic. Attackers exploit the weakest link, gain persistence, and use that access to escalate into larger systems. By the time victims realize what has happened, the dominoes have already fallen.

The Human Factor in IoT Catastrophes

Beyond technical vulnerabilities lies perhaps the most challenging aspect of IoT security: human behavior. Users consistently prioritize convenience over security, often without understanding the trade-offs they're making. The default password crisis exemplifies this perfectly while security experts have been warning about weak passwords for decades, millions of IoT devices remain protected by credentials like "admin/admin" or "123456."

The problem is compounded by the invisibility of IoT security. Unlike a traditional computer, which displays security warnings and prompts users to install updates, many IoT devices operate silently in the background. A smart thermostat might be compromised for months without the homeowner noticing any change in functionality. This invisibility means that breaches can persist undetected, giving attackers time to establish persistence and plan larger attacks. Consumer education represents both a critical need and an enormous challenge. How do you explain to someone buying a smart doorbell that they're potentially creating an entry point for cybercriminals? How do you convey that their $50 security camera might compromise their entire home network? The gap between user understanding and actual risk creates a persistent vulnerability that no amount of technical security can fully address.

Anatomies of IoT catastrophes reveal a consistent pattern. They begin at the periphery with weak devices built for convenience, not security. From there, attackers pivoted inward, exploiting connectivity to access larger and more critical systems. The cascade of failures that follows often spans personal, corporate, and national boundaries. A hacked baby monitor may seem trivial until it becomes part of a botnet that cripples the internet. A compromised smart car may be a curiosity until attackers weaponize fleets to cause mass accidents. A vulnerable hospital sensor may be overlooked until it leads to loss of life.

The rise of IoT has blurred the boundary between digital and physical worlds. This means that catastrophes no longer remain confined to cyberspace; they spill into streets, hospitals, factories, and homes. The anatomy of an IoT catastrophe is, therefore, not merely technical it is human. It disrupts trust, endangers lives, and destabilizes societies.

The scale of potential IoT catastrophes continues to grow as our dependence on connected devices deepens. Smart cities, autonomous vehicles, remote surgery, and industrial automation all represent expanding attack surfaces where the consequences of failure become increasingly severe. We are rapidly approaching a point where IoT security failures won't just inconvenience users; they will reshape how societies function and interact.

As we look ahead, the lessons from past breaches demand attention. Weak links will always exist. Domino effects will always threaten to spiral out of control. And real-world breaches will continue to expose the fragility of our interconnected world. The challenge is not in recognizing that catastrophes are possible as they already have happened but in preventing the next one from being far worse. The anatomy of an IoT catastrophe teaches us that in our rush to connect everything, we have created a world where everything is vulnerable. The question is no longer whether catastrophic IoT failures will occur, but how we will respond when they inevitably do. Our preparation for that inevitable moment will determine whether the next IoT catastrophe becomes a manageable incident or a civilization-altering event.

Chapter Four

Cyber Armageddon Scenarios

When Cities Go Dark: Critical Infrastructure at Risk

Imagine this: it's a warm evening in midsummer, and a city of ten million is humming with activity. Commuters are heading home, restaurants are filling with patrons, and hospitals are running at full capacity. Children play in air-conditioned homes while their parents stream entertainment on smart TVs. Elderly residents depend on connected medical devices to monitor their vital signs. The city breathes through an intricate network of sensors, switches, and automated systems that regulate everything from traffic flow to air quality.

Suddenly, without warning, the power grid collapses. Traffic lights freeze red, plunging intersections into chaos. Subway trains grind to a halt between stations, trapping passengers in suffocating tunnels. Hospitals switch to backup generators, but only for critical wards, dialysis machines shut down, ventilators switch to battery power, and operating rooms go dark mid-surgery. Within minutes, the vibrant city is reduced to paralysis. Cell towers fail as their backup power depletes. ATMs stop dispensing cash. Elevators trap people between floors in high-rise buildings. Water treatment plants lose power, threatening the safety of millions of gallons of drinking water.

This is not the plot of a dystopian film. It is a plausible consequence of IoT vulnerabilities embedded in modern power grids. The electrical grid is no longer a closed system of analog switches and human operators. Today, it depends on thousands of IoT sensors to balance loads, detect faults, and optimize efficiency. These devices, connected meters, smart transformers, automated controls, and distributed energy resources, make the grid more responsive and efficient, but they also expand its attack surface exponentially. If even a fraction of those sensors are compromised, attackers could feed false data into the system, causing protective systems to malfunction and forcing cascading blackouts across entire regions.

The 2015 cyberattack on Ukraine's power grid provides a sobering real-world example. Hackers, believed to be state-sponsored, infiltrated control systems and shut off electricity to more than 230,000 residents. The attackers demonstrated sophisticated knowledge of industrial control systems, using custom malware to overwrite firmware and render backup systems inoperable. Operators were locked out of their systems as attackers remotely disabled power substations, some for hours. While this incident did not involve IoT in the consumer sense, it illustrated how invisible cyberattacks could plunge entire populations into darkness with surgical precision.

If similar tactics were combined with modern IoT vulnerabilities, compromised smart meters providing false consumption data, hacked grid sensors reporting phantom equipment failures, or corrupted weather monitoring systems feeding incorrect data into renewable energy forecasting, the results could be catastrophically worse. The distributed nature of IoT means that attackers would have millions of potential entry points rather than the handful that existed in Ukraine's centralized system.

And electricity is only one piece of the puzzle. Water systems, traffic management networks, emergency services, telecommunications, and even waste management all depend on IoT to function efficiently. In 2021, hackers attempted to poison the water supply of Oldsmar, Florida, by breaching its control systems and adjusting chemical levels from 100 parts per million to 11,100 parts per million a potentially lethal concentration. Though quickly detected by an alert operator, the incident exposed the fragility of modern infrastructure. A single compromised sensor or controller could have endangered thousands of lives without anyone realizing it until people began falling ill.

The interdependencies make the situation even more precarious. When power fails, water pumping stations stop working. When water systems fail, hospitals cannot maintain sterile conditions. When transportation networks collapse, emergency responders cannot reach those in need. When communications fail, coordination becomes impossible. Each system's failure accelerates the collapse of others, creating a domino effect that transforms isolated incidents into civilization-threatening catastrophes.

Now picture an attack that deliberately combines these elements: a coordinated assault that begins with a blackout disabling hospitals and communications, followed by contaminated water supplies sowing panic, and culminates with gridlocked transportation paralyzing response efforts. In this scenario, the cyberattack itself remains invisible to most victims, yet its effects are as tangible as any conventional act of war. Cities may not burn, but they collapse nonetheless, undone not by bombs but by corrupted code running on devices once dismissed as mundane appliances.

From Homes to Hospitals: Life-Threatening Attacks

While critical infrastructure represents the most visible target for cyber-Armageddon, catastrophes can also begin in the most personal and intimate of places: our homes, our bodies, and the medical facilities we trust with our lives. The devices designed to keep us comfortable, connected, and even alive can, under hostile control, become weapons turned against their very purpose.

In 2017, the U.S. Food and Drug Administration recalled nearly half a million pacemakers because they were vulnerable to remote hacking. Security researchers demonstrated that attackers within radio range could alter pacing commands, change heart rate settings, or systematically drain the battery without a patient's knowledge or consent. Though no mass attack occurred, the possibility was terrifying: an invisible hand reaching into the human body, capable of ending life with a few lines of code. The victim would likely never know they were under attack until their heart began beating irregularly or stopped entirely.

As healthcare embraces IoT more deeply, these opportunities for life-threatening sabotage multiply exponentially. Insulin pumps can be hacked to deliver fatal doses of medication. Wireless patient monitors can be manipulated to hide critical symptoms or trigger false alarms that overwhelm medical staff. Connected surgical tools could malfunction during operations. Even seemingly benign devices like smart hospital beds could be weaponized to cause falls or pressure injuries in vulnerable patients.

The convergence of ransomware and healthcare IoT presents an especially nightmarish scenario. Ransomware has already demonstrated the human cost of cyberattacks on hospitals. In

2017, the WannaCry ransomware crippled the UK's National Health Service, forcing hospitals to cancel thousands of surgeries, divert ambulances to unaffected facilities, and delay treatment for patients with life-threatening conditions. The attack caused an estimated £92 million in damages and untold human suffering as people were denied critical care.

While WannaCry spread primarily through traditional computer networks, security experts warn that insecure medical IoT devices could serve as vectors in future attacks and make them far more devastating. If hospital networks are infiltrated through connected devices, attackers could move beyond simply encrypting files to directly interfering with life-critical equipment. Imagine ransomware that doesn't just lock computer screens but actually disables ventilators, dialysis machines, and cardiac monitors until payment is made. In such scenarios, ransomware evolves from financial crime to outright terrorism, with human lives being held hostage.

Even our homes, once considered sanctuaries, are not immune to these intimate betrayals of trust. Smart locks can be remotely opened to allow intruders access while families sleep. Security cameras can be hijacked to spy on residents or disabled to provide cover for physical crimes. Smart thermostats can be manipulated to create dangerously hot or cold conditions, particularly threatening elderly residents or young children. Connected smoke detectors can be silenced during actual fires, while smart garage doors can trap residents inside or allow unauthorized access. In one particularly chilling demonstration, security researchers hacked into a smart baby monitor, using it to broadcast a stranger's voice into a nursery, terrifying parents and potentially traumatizing children. In another case, attackers hijacked smart thermostats across multiple homes simultaneously, causing extreme temperature fluctuations that forced residents to evacuate in the middle of winter. While such incidents may seem small in scale compared to citywide blackouts, they illustrate the deep personal and psychological nature of IoT catastrophes. A blackout may inconvenience millions, but a hacked medical device or a compromised smart home strikes at the intimate core of human security and violates the very spaces where people should feel safest.

Connected vehicles represent another critical front line in the convergence of consumer convenience and life-threatening risk. The 2015 Jeep Cherokee hack revealed that modern cars are no longer primarily mechanical machines but computers on wheels, as vulnerable to digital attacks as laptops or routers. In their demonstration, security researchers remotely disabled the brakes and transmission of the Jeep while it was traveling on a busy highway, forcing Chrysler to recall 1.4 million vehicles and issue emergency software patches. Extrapolate this scenario to a future where autonomous vehicles dominate highways and city streets. A coordinated attack on thousands of connected cars could simultaneously disable transportation across entire metropolitan areas, cause mass accidents, and completely overwhelm emergency response systems. Attackers could target specific vehicle types, geographic regions, or even individual passengers, turning the promise of safer transportation into a weapon of unprecedented precision and scale. The line between consumer convenience and public catastrophe blurs when IoT vehicles are weaponized against the people they were designed to protect.

What makes these scenarios particularly chilling is their invisibility and intimacy. Patients do not notice when their pacemaker's firmware has been quietly corrupted. Drivers do not realize when their cars have been recruited into a botnet, waiting for activation commands. Families may never suspect that their smart refrigerator has been compromised and is now part of a surveillance network or that their connected doorbell is being used to map their daily routines for criminal exploitation. The attack remains completely unseen until the consequences erupt into the physical world and by then, it may be far too late to prevent tragedy.

Economic Havoc in a Connected Marketplace

If cities are going dark and hospitals under siege illustrate the immediate human toll of IoT catastrophes, the economic consequences reveal their potential to reshape civilization itself. The modern global economy depends on an incredibly delicate web of logistics, manufacturing, finance, and commerce all increasingly powered by IoT devices that optimize efficiency but also create systemic vulnerabilities.

Disruptions in this interconnected web could create economic chaos rivaling the Great Depression or the collapse of entire civilizations.

Considering the complexity of global supply chains, the arteries through which modern commerce flows. From massive shipping ports where cranes are guided by IoT sensors to vast warehouses where millions of packages are sorted by automated systems, connected devices track cargo locations, optimize storage algorithms, monitor environmental conditions, and coordinate just-in-time deliveries across continents. A coordinated attack on these systems could simultaneously delay shipments of essential goods, food, medical supplies, energy resources, and industrial components across multiple continents.

During the COVID-19 pandemic, even relatively small supply chain disruptions caused widespread shortages, empty store shelves, and economic ripple effects that lasted for years. Now imagine those disruptions not as accidents of circumstance, but as deliberate, precisely timed, and globally coordinated sabotage. Manufacturing plants grind to halt as IoT sensors provide false readings about inventory levels and quality control. Shipping ports become clogged with containers whose tracking systems have been corrupted, making it impossible to determine contents or destinations. Retailers struggle to maintain basic inventories as their automated ordering systems are fed false data about demand

and availability. The result would not be merely inconvenient but complete economic paralysis affecting billions of people.

Financial markets present equally catastrophic vulnerabilities. Modern trading floors and stock exchanges increasingly rely on high-speed networks of IoT sensors and automated trading systems that process billions of transactions per second. These systems depend on real-time data feeds from connected devices monitoring everything from weather patterns that affect agricultural commodities to shipping traffic that influences oil prices to consumer behavior tracked through IoT devices in retail environments.

A sophisticated cyberattack exploiting IoT vulnerabilities could feed false data into these systems on a massive scale, triggering algorithmic trading responses that create cascading market crashes. Imagine attackers simultaneously manipulating weather sensors to suggest crop failures, shipping sensors to indicate supply disruptions, and consumer IoT devices to fabricate demand signals. The resulting market movements could erase trillions of dollars in value within hours, triggering margin calls, forcing pension fund liquidations, and potentially collapsing entire national economies.

Even relatively short disruptions could have lasting consequences. The 2010 "Flash Crash," caused by a single large, automated trade, wiped out nearly $1 trillion in market value in minutes before recovering. A deliberate attack using compromised IoT data could create multiple flash crashes simultaneously across different markets and asset classes, with recovery becoming impossible as investor confidence evaporates entirely. The ransomware attack on Colonial Pipeline in 2021 provides a preview of how cyber sabotage can create immediate economic havoc. Though not strictly an IoT attack, it highlighted the catastrophic potential of digital attacks against physical infrastructure. The pipeline shutdown forced fuel shortages across the Eastern United States, caused panic buying that emptied gas stations, led to flight cancellations as airports ran out of jet fuel, and created ripple effects throughout the economy as transportation costs soared.

If attackers had simultaneously targeted IoT-enabled monitoring systems across multiple pipelines, refineries, and distribution networks, the economic fallout could have been exponentially worse, potentially triggering a national energy crisis that collapsed trucking, aviation, and manufacturing sectors simultaneously. The psychological impact alone of consumers losing faith in the stability of essential services could have created panic that amplified the economic damage far beyond the immediate physical disruptions.

Leading economists have begun warning of a potential "cyber pandemic," a cascading series of IoT-based attacks that spread across industries and continents as quickly as a biological virus, but with the deliberate malice of human intelligence guiding their evolution. Unlike natural disasters, which are geographically localized and temporally limited, a cyber pandemic could simultaneously affect multiple economic sectors across the globe, creating interconnected failures that amplify each other's impact.

Imagine an attack scenario that begins with compromised shipping sensors in Asian manufacturing hubs, spreads through European logistics networks as containers with corrupted tracking data create customs delays and finally disrupts North American financial markets as commodity prices swing wildly in response to false supply signals all within a matter of hours. The result would be a synchronized global economic shock with no historical precedent, potentially triggering the collapse of international trade relationships that took decades to build.

The long-term consequences of such economic havoc extend far beyond immediate financial losses. If consumers lose faith in digital commerce and return to cash-based transactions, if businesses abandon global supply chains in favor of local production, if governments impose strict controls on IoT devices to prevent economic sabotage, the very foundations of the digital economy could crumble. Trust is the ultimate currency of our connected world, and once it is destroyed, the costs of rebuilding it may dwarf even the worst financial losses from the attacks themselves.

Cyber Armageddon does not require mushroom clouds, missile strikes, or invading armies. It requires only the silent compromise of billions of devices we have woven into the fabric of modern civilization. Cities can go dark, hospitals can falter, economies can unravel, and societies can collapse, all without a single conventional shot being fired. The Internet of Things, while representing one of humanity's greatest technological achievements, has also inadvertently created the most expansive and vulnerable battlefield in human history, one where the weapons are invisible, the attackers can remain anonymous, and the casualties can be simultaneously personal and civilizational.

The scenarios outlined in this chapter are not distant science fiction or paranoid fantasies. They are logical extensions of real-world incidents that have already occurred: Ukraine's power grid attacks that left hundreds of thousands in darkness, compromised vehicle systems that forced massive recalls, WannaCry's ransomware that shut down hospitals across continents, Colonial Pipeline's disruption that created nationwide fuel shortages. Each incident served as both a warning and a proof of concept, demonstrating the growing potential for cyber catastrophes to bridge the digital and physical worlds with devastating consequences.

What makes these potential catastrophes especially terrifying is their multidimensional nature. They strike simultaneously at the most personal level our homes where we seek comfort, our bodies that we trust to medical devices, and our intimate spaces where we should feel safe and at the most systemic level, our cities' infrastructure, our global economy, our international relationships, and our faith in technological progress itself. The anatomy of cyber-Armageddon is not a single cataclysmic event but rather a convergence of countless smaller crises, each amplifying the others until individual failures cascade into civilizational collapse.

The rise of IoT has given humanity unprecedented power to connect every aspect of our lives, automate countless processes that once required human oversight, and optimize systems in ways that seemed impossible just decades ago. But this same interconnectedness has also created the possibility of unprecedented catastrophe, where the compromise of seemingly insignificant devices, a smart thermostat, a connected sensor, and a wireless medical monitor, can trigger chains of events that threaten millions of lives and reshape the global order.

The question facing humanity is not whether these IoT-enabled catastrophes are possible, they demonstrably are. The question is whether our response will be characterized by resilience and proactive defense or by reactive crisis management after disasters have already been struck. Whether the future is defined by the promise of connectivity or the specter of systemic collapse will depend on how seriously we heed the lessons embedded in these scenarios before they evolve from theoretical possibilities into historical realities that future generations study as turning points in human civilization.

Chapter Five

Espionage in the Age of Smart Things

The twenty-first century has normalized something that would have seemed outlandish even a generation ago: voluntary surveillance in our most private spaces. Smart TVs, voice-activated speakers, internet-connected security cameras, baby monitors, and thermostats have become household staples. Yet these conveniences double as ready-made channels for espionage. Unlike the bugged lamps or concealed microphones of Cold War lore, modern devices are purchased willingly by consumers, installed with enthusiasm, and connected directly to the global internet. For intelligence agencies and cybercriminals alike, the espionage potential is unprecedented.

The transformation has been remarkably swift. In 2010, fewer than 10 billion devices were connected to the internet globally. By 2025, that number is projected to exceed 75 billion, with the majority being consumer IoT devices. Each represents a potential surveillance endpoint, creating an espionage landscape that dwarfs anything imagined during the height of the Cold War. Where the East German Stasi employed roughly 100,000 agents and informants to monitor 16 million citizens a ratio that shocked the world modern IoT creates the possibility of ubiquitous surveillance with minimal human involvement.

In 2017, WikiLeaks released the infamous "Vault 7" documents, a massive leak of Central Intelligence Agency (CIA) cyber tools. Among the revelations was "Weeping Angel," a program designed to turn certain Samsung smart TVs into covert microphones. Even when appearing to be switched off, compromised TVs could record conversations in a room and transmit them back to intelligence handlers. The program was developed in partnership with Britain's MI5, demonstrating how IoT espionage has become a collaborative effort among allied intelligence agencies. While the CIA's tools were intended for espionage against foreign adversaries, the leaks exposed a larger reality: any internet-connected microphone or camera could be transformed into a listening device.

Voice-activated assistants have proven particularly vulnerable to exploitation. Amazon's Alexa, Google Assistant, and Apple's Siri are designed to listen continuously for wake words, creating a persistent audio monitoring capability in millions of homes. Security researchers have demonstrated "skill squatting" attacks, where malicious voice applications mimic legitimate services to capture sensitive information. In one documented case, researchers created fake banking skills that could trick users into revealing account information, passwords, and personal details. The devices' always-listening nature means that even conversations not intended for the assistant may be captured and transmitted.

The implications extend beyond intelligence agencies. Criminal groups have repeatedly exploited IoT consumer devices for surveillance. In 2014, hackers infiltrated thousands of unsecured baby monitors, using them to spy on children and their families. Victims reported hearing strange voices issuing commands to their children through the monitors. Though technically crude compared to state-level tools, such incidents underscored the same point: IoT had placed microphones and cameras in millions of private spaces, and attackers needed only minimal skill to exploit them.

The Ring doorbell security scandal of 2019 further illustrated the vulnerability of consumer IoT. Amazon's Ring devices, marketed as home security solutions, were found to have lax security practices that allowed unauthorized access to video feeds. Hundreds of incidents emerged where strangers gained access to Ring cameras, speaking to children through the devices and watching families in their most intimate moments. While Amazon claimed these were isolated incidents resulting from password reuse, security researchers discovered fundamental vulnerabilities in the devices themselves.

Unlike traditional espionage, which required physical infiltration, IoT surveillance can be scaled globally. With automated scanning tools, attackers can identify vulnerable devices by the thousands. Shodan, a search engine for internet-connected devices, has been repeatedly used by researchers and criminals to locate unsecured cameras and smart home devices. In one study, researchers discovered more than 15,000 insecure baby monitors are publicly accessible online. For spies and adversaries, this is not mere eavesdropping but mass surveillance at negligible cost.

The psychological impact of ubiquitous surveillance extends beyond immediate privacy concerns. The knowledge that smart devices might be compromised creates a chilling effect on private conversations and behaviors. Families report moving sensitive discussions away from smart speakers, covering cameras when not in use, and feeling perpetually watched in their own homes. This erosion of private space represents a fundamental shift in how societies function, reminiscent of authoritarian surveillance states but implemented through commercial consumer products.

The erosion of privacy at the consumer level feeds into broader espionage concerns. Conversations captured in living rooms may include sensitive corporate discussions, political opinions, or private vulnerabilities that can later be exploited. The "spy in the living room" is not just a metaphor; it is the baseline reality of modern espionage. Where once intelligence agencies relied on human sources or covert bugs, they now find households filled with microphones, cameras, and data streams voluntarily installed by the very people being surveilled.

Corporate Espionage Through Connected Devices

If consumer IoT has created a fertile ground for domestic surveillance, corporate IoT has expanded the battlefield into boardrooms, offices, and factories. Espionage has always thrived where trade secrets and intellectual property are at stake, but the digitalization of business processes and the rise of IoT within them has made corporate espionage both easier and more devastating. The scale of corporate IoT adoption has been staggering. Manufacturing companies deploy thousands of sensors to monitor production lines, optimize efficiency, and predict equipment failures. Office buildings integrate smart lighting, HVAC systems, and security cameras into comprehensive building management platforms. Retail chains use IoT to track inventory, monitor customer behavior, and manage supply chains. Each of these systems generates valuable intelligence about business operations, strategies, and vulnerabilities.

One of the clearest demonstrations of this came in the form of supply chain infiltration. In 2018, Bloomberg published a controversial report alleging that Chinese operatives had inserted tiny microchips into hardware supplied to major

American firms, including Apple and Amazon. Though the details remain disputed, the broader concern is legitimate: IoT and embedded devices sourced from global supply chains may carry hidden espionage functions. Unlike traditional malware, which can be detected and patched, hardware-level compromises are nearly impossible to identify and eliminate once deployed.

The sophistication of supply chain attacks has evolved considerably. Modern threats involve compromising legitimate manufacturer systems to inject malicious code during the production process, creating authentic-appearing devices with hidden backdoors. The 2020 SolarWinds attack demonstrated how software supply chains could be weaponized for espionage, and similar techniques are increasingly being applied to hardware and IoT device manufacturing. Smart offices are equally vulnerable. Internet-connected printers, conference room cameras, and wireless presentation systems have all been exploited to exfiltrate data. In one case, security researchers uncovered vulnerabilities in networked printers that allowed attackers to steal documents directly from the printing queue. These printers, often overlooked in security assessments, maintain local copies of all printed documents and can be accessed remotely through network vulnerabilities.

Another study demonstrated how compromised wireless projectors in corporate boardrooms could be used to capture confidential presentations. These devices, designed for convenience in business meetings, often lack robust security controls and can be exploited to record presentations, capture screenshots, or even activate hidden cameras and microphones. The Cisco WebEx vulnerability disclosed in 2020 showed how video conferencing systems could be exploited to spy on corporate meetings, giving attackers access to strategic discussions and confidential information.

The rise of smart badges and employee tracking systems has created new avenues for corporate espionage. Many companies now issue IoT-enabled identification badges that track employee movements throughout office buildings, ostensibly for security and efficiency purposes. However, these systems generate detailed maps of employee behavior, meeting patterns, and social networks within organizations. Compromising such systems provides adversaries with unprecedented insight into corporate hierarchies, key personnel, and operational patterns.

Factories and industrial settings, increasingly reliant on IoT for automation, present a different but equally troubling target. Espionage in this context often centers on stealing proprietary manufacturing processes or designs. In 2019, hackers targeted Norsk Hydro, a major aluminum producer, in a ransomware attack that disrupted operations worldwide. While the incident was framed as criminal extortion, investigators suggested that industrial espionage groups were closely observing how the attack unfolded, learning how IoT-linked operational technology could be leveraged for strategic advantage.

Industrial IoT systems often contain highly sensitive intellectual property embedded in their operational parameters. Production line sensors capture data about manufacturing processes, quality control measures, and efficiency optimizations that represent years of research and development investment. Competitors or nation-state actors who gain access to this information can reverse engineering proprietary processes or identify competitive advantages without investing in their own research. The automotive industry provides a particularly stark example of IoT-enabled corporate espionage risks. Modern vehicles contain dozens of IoT sensors and communication systems that generate detailed data about performance, efficiency, and design characteristics. When Tesla vehicles began operating in Chinese markets, concerns emerged about whether the detailed sensor data being collected could reveal proprietary information about Tesla's manufacturing processes, battery technology, and autonomous driving algorithms.

IoT's role in corporate espionage extends beyond simple data theft. It enables persistent surveillance. For instance, a compromised office security camera may not just capture one meeting, but months of employee comings and goings, identifying key personnel, patterns of collaboration, or even potential insider threats. In the hands of nation-state actors, such information can be weaponized not only to steal intellectual property but to map organizational vulnerabilities for later exploitation. The financial sector has experienced particular targeting through IoT-enabled corporate espionage. Smart building systems in financial institutions have been compromised to gather intelligence about trading strategies, merger discussions, and regulatory responses. The 2016 Bangladesh Bank heist, while not directly involving IoT, demonstrated how cyber attackers could steal not just money but detailed information about international financial networks and security procedures.

Ultimately, IoT has transformed corporate espionage from a high-cost, high-risk endeavor reliant on insider bribes, covert photography, or physical infiltration into a largely remote, scalable operation. The stakes are immense. Intellectual property theft already costs the global economy an estimated $600 billion annually, much of it attributed to cyber-enabled espionage. As businesses continue to adopt IoT, the risk is not just economic but strategic: adversaries may acquire the technological edge not through innovation but through invisible theft facilitated by connected devices.

Nation-State Espionage in a Connected World

At the highest level, IoT espionage becomes a matter of national security. Nation-states have long sought to penetrate each other's communications, but IoT has dramatically expanded the field of play. Where once espionage was limited to phone taps or intercepted cables, it now encompasses billions of IoT endpoints: smart city sensors, connected vehicles, medical devices, and industrial control systems. Each is a potential entry point for state-backed spies.

The scale of nation-state IoT espionage operations is difficult to comprehend. Intelligence agencies now contend with data streams from billions of devices, requiring unprecedented computational resources to process and analyze. The National Security Agency's Utah Data Center, with its estimated storage capacity of yottabytes, represents the kind of infrastructure necessary to make sense of IoT-generated intelligence on a global scale.

China's Belt and Road Initiative, for example, has raised persistent concerns about the dual-use nature of the IoT infrastructure it exports. Smart city technologies, traffic systems, surveillance cameras, and public Wi-Fi installed by Chinese companies in dozens of countries could, critics argue, serve as global surveillance platforms. While these systems improve urban efficiency, they also centralize vast amounts of sensitive data in infrastructure controlled by foreign vendors, creating opportunities for intelligence collection at scale. The strategic implications of this infrastructure penetration are profound. Smart city systems capture information about population movements, economic activity, social patterns, and infrastructure vulnerabilities that would have been impossible to collect through traditional espionage methods. When multiplied across dozens of countries, this creates a global intelligence network of unprecedented scope and sophistication.

Russia, too, has embraced IoT-enabled espionage. The 2017 NotPetya attack, widely attributed to Russian state actors, crippled Ukrainian infrastructure and multinational corporations alike. Though technically framed as sabotage, NotPetya's effects also included massive data exfiltration. By compromising IoT-enabled logistics systems, attackers were able to map global supply chains, a goldmine of intelligence with both economic and military applications. The Russian approach to IoT espionage often blends traditional intelligence gathering with information warfare objectives. The compromise of IoT devices serves not just to collect intelligence but to create narratives and influence operations. Smart home devices compromised by Russian actors have been used to amplify disinformation campaigns, turning private communications into vectors for propaganda and social manipulation.

The United States and its allies have likewise integrated IoT into intelligence operations. Documents leaked by Edward Snowden revealed extensive U.S. surveillance of global communications networks, and while those disclosures predated the full explosion of IoT, they signaled a trend: intelligence agencies are willing and able to exploit any digital channel. With billions of IoT devices now transmitting data daily, the opportunities for collection dwarf anything imagined in earlier eras.

American intelligence agencies have developed sophisticated capabilities for exploiting IoT devices manufactured by adversary nations. The classification of Chinese telecommunications equipment as security risks reflects broader concerns about embedded espionage capabilities in IoT devices. However, the U.S. also maintains significant IoT intelligence collection capabilities, as revealed through various leaks and official disclosures about programs targeting foreign IoT infrastructure. The Five Eyes intelligence alliance comprising the United States, United Kingdom, Canada, Australia, and New Zealand has coordinated extensively on IoT espionage operations. This collaboration allows for global IoT surveillance capabilities that span multiple jurisdictions and legal frameworks, creating comprehensive intelligence collection networks that individual nations could not achieve alone.

The blurred line between espionage and sabotage is particularly troubling in the IoT domain. When a state actor compromises a smart grid sensor, is the goal to spy on energy usage, to map vulnerabilities for future attacks, or to prepare for sabotage in the event of conflict? The same applies to healthcare IoT: stealing patient data may be espionage, but disabling medical devices veers into open aggression. This ambiguity complicates international norms. Unlike nuclear weapons or traditional military tools, IoT espionage tools operate in a legal and ethical gray zone, making deterrence difficult. The concept of "preparation of the battlefield" has taken on new meaning in the IoT era. Nation-states routinely compromise IoT infrastructure not for immediate intelligence gathering but to establish persistent access for future operations. This creates a situation where potential adversaries maintain dormant capabilities within each other's critical infrastructure, creating hair-trigger scenarios where espionage operations could quickly escalate to destructive attacks.

Perhaps the most alarming frontier is biometric and personal data harvested via IoT. Fitness trackers, smartwatches, and medical monitors generate streams of information that, when aggregated, reveal not just health details but movement patterns, relationships, and routines. In 2018, fitness app Strava published a global "heat map" of user activity, inadvertently exposing the locations of U.S. military bases abroad as soldiers' running routes lit up the map. This incident underscored how seemingly trivial consumer IoT data can become invaluable intelligence for nation-states. The intelligence value of aggregated IoT data extends far beyond individual surveillance. Nation-states can use IoT data to understand economic trends, predict social unrest, identify key infrastructure vulnerabilities, and map the relationships between critical personnel. The Chinese social credit system provides a glimpse of how IoT data can be systematically collected and analyzed to create comprehensive profiles of entire populations.

Medical IoT devices present particularly sensitive intelligence targets. Pacemakers, insulin pumps, and other implanted devices not only generate health data but can reveal information about political leaders, military personnel, and other high-value intelligence targets. The assassination of a foreign leader through a compromised medical device would represent a new category of state-sponsored violence enabled by IoT vulnerabilities. The cumulative effect is clear: IoT has expanded espionage beyond the realm of elite spies and classified operations. It now pervades civilian life, corporate activity, and global infrastructure. Nation-states that exploit this reality gain unprecedented visibility into their adversaries' societies and economies. Those that fail to secure their IoT ecosystems risk not just privacy breaches but strategic disadvantage on the world stage.

Espionage in the age of smart things is not marked by dramatic cloak-and-dagger moments but by silent, persistent infiltration. The microphones and cameras in our homes, the connected devices in our offices, and the sensors embedded in our cities all represent channels through which information can be siphoned away.

The post-2000s era has proven that espionage is no longer confined to classified documents and secret meetings. It is embedded in the ordinary: a compromised smart TV, a hacked conference camera, a vulnerable supply chain sensor. For consumers, this means that privacy is perpetually at risk. For corporations, it means that intellectual property is constantly exposed. For nations, it means that sovereignty itself is challenged by invisible incursions. The democratization of espionage through IoT has fundamentally altered the balance of power in intelligence gathering. Where only major nation-states could conduct sophisticated surveillance operations, now smaller countries, criminal organizations, and even individual actors can access powerful espionage capabilities through IoT exploitation. This proliferation of espionage capabilities creates unpredictable risks and makes attribution increasingly difficult.

The economic implications of IoT-enabled espionage are staggering. Beyond the direct costs of intellectual property theft, companies must now invest billions in securing IoT infrastructure that was originally designed for convenience and efficiency rather than security. The hidden costs of espionage lost competitive advantages, compromised strategies, and eroded trust, may ultimately exceed the visible economic damage. Unlike the overt catastrophes of blackouts or ransomware attacks, IoT espionage rarely makes headlines in the same dramatic fashion. Its power lies in subtlety, knowledge quietly stolen, vulnerabilities quietly mapped, influence quietly exerted. But this subtlety does not lessen its danger. On the contrary, espionage facilitated by IoT may be the most strategically consequential dimension of the IoT Armageddon, shaping not just immediate crises but the balance of power in the decades to come.

The invisible intelligence war enabled by IoT represents a paradigm shift in how power operates in the modern world. Information has always been powered, but never before has so much information been so accessible to so many actors. The nations, corporations, and individuals who master the art of IoT espionage while protecting themselves from it will hold decisive advantages in the conflicts and competitions that define the twenty-first century.

Chapter Six

The Rise of IoT Botnets

The rise of botnets is one of the most defining features of the modern cyber threat landscape, and no episode brought the issue into sharper focus than the Mirai attack of 2016. For years, security experts had warned that insecure Internet of Things (IoT) devices routers, IP cameras, DVRs, and more could be weaponized on a massive scale. But it was Mirai that proved the point with devastating clarity.

Created by three college students, Mirai spread by scanning the internet for devices with default usernames and passwords. Once infected, these devices became part of a vast botnet, an army of compromised machines capable of acting in unison under remote command. The scale was staggering. At its peak, Mirai had enslaved over 600,000 devices. The botnet's most infamous strike came in September 2016, when it launched a distributed denial-of-service (DDoS) attack against Dyn, a major DNS provider. The attack temporarily crippled internet access across the United States and parts of Europe, taking down sites like Twitter, Netflix, and Reddit.

Mirai was a watershed moment not just because of its technical novelty it was, in many ways, a relatively simple piece of malware but because it demonstrated the raw power of IoT botnets. Devices designed for convenience and connectivity have been turned into a digital weapon capable of shaking the foundations of the global internet. What made Mirai particularly alarming was its accessibility. Once the original creators were caught, the source code was released publicly online. This democratized botnet creation, enabling criminals, hacktivists, and state-backed groups alike to adapt Mirai's code for their own purposes. In the years that followed, countless Mirai variants appeared, each with slight modifications but the same fundamental strategy: exploit insecure IoT devices to build massive networks of compromised endpoints.

The lesson should have been clear: insecure IoT devices pose systemic risks. Yet, despite the headlines, manufacturers largely continued to ship products with poor security. Default passwords, weak firmware protections, and lack of patching mechanisms persisted. As a result, Mirai was not the end of the story, it was the beginning.

Anatomy of a Botnet Army

To understand why botnets have flourished, it is important to examine how they form and evolve. At their core, botnets rely on scale. Unlike traditional malware campaigns targeting a handful of high-value systems, botnets thrive by compromising vast numbers of low-value devices. A single infected webcam may not matter, but a million compromised webcams working together can bring down national-scale infrastructure.

The process begins with infection. Most IoT botnets spread by scanning the internet for devices with known vulnerabilities commonly default credentials, outdated firmware, or open ports. Once identified, these devices are compromised and connected to a command-and-control (C2) infrastructure. From there, they await instructions: launch a DDoS attack, send spam, mine cryptocurrency, or serve as entry points for further infiltration.

Different types of devices have proven especially susceptible. Consumer routers are among the most common targets, both because of their ubiquity and because many are left in their factory-default state. IP cameras and DVRs are also prime targets, particularly those mass-produced by manufacturers with little incentive to prioritize security. Increasingly, industrial IoT devices, such as smart meters and control systems, are being added to the list of botnet prey.

Botnets are not static. They evolve as defenders respond. Early IoT botnets like Bashlite (also known as Gafgyt) focused almost exclusively on launching DDoS attacks. Later botnets like Hajime introduced more sophistication. Hajime, discovered in 2016, spread using similar techniques to Mirai but introduced peer-to-peer communication rather than relying on a central command server. This made it more resilient: even if some nodes were taken down, the network could continue to operate. Hajime's authors claimed it was a "white hat" botnet, designed to secure vulnerable devices against Mirai, but its ambiguous motives highlighted a broader trend, botnets were becoming more advanced, stealthier, and harder to dismantle.

Mozi, first observed in 2019, took the evolution further. Built on peer-to-peer architecture, Mozi became the largest known IoT botnet by 2020, with an estimated 500,000 compromised devices under its control. Mozi's capabilities extended beyond DDoS; it could deliver payloads, execute arbitrary code, and persist across reboots. Researchers noted that Mozi adapted quickly to defensive measures, updating itself and using advanced obfuscation techniques to avoid detection.

The diversity of purposes has also expanded. Beyond classic DDoS, modern IoT botnets have been repurposed for cryptocurrency mining, data theft, and even ransomware delivery. Some botnets operate as "for hire" services, rented out on underground markets to criminals who lack the technical skills to build their own. The commodification of botnets mirrors broader trends in cybercrime: professionalization, specialization, and commercialization.

The anatomy of an IoT botnet army thus reflects both technical and economic realities. IoT devices are cheap, insecure, and everywhere. The cost of infection is low, but the collective power is immense. As long as these conditions persist, botnets will remain a dominant feature of the cyber threat landscape.

Botnets as Weapons of Geopolitics

While Mirai and its successors began as criminal tools, the strategic implications for nation-states were not lost on intelligence and military planners. An IoT botnet is not just a nuisance for website operators, it can be a weapon of geopolitical significance.

Consider the potential of a million-device botnet in the hands of a state actor. Such a botnet could be used to disrupt critical infrastructure, overwhelm government communication channels, or sow chaos during political crises. It could serve as a diversion, masking more targeted espionage operations. It could even be unleashed as a form of digital coercion, signaling capability without resorting to overt military force.

Evidence suggests that some states have already embraced these tactics. Security researchers have linked several large-scale DDoS campaigns to nation-state actors, often coinciding with political tensions. In 2017, Estonia experienced waves of cyberattacks believed to be linked to geopolitical disputes with Russia, and while not all of these attacks were traced to IoT botnets specifically, the use of distributed attack infrastructure demonstrated the potential role of botnets in statecraft.

Mozi, in particular, raised alarms because of its persistence and adaptability. Chinese researchers noted that Mozi was disproportionately active in regions aligned with strategic Chinese interests, leading some analysts to speculate that the botnet might be leveraged, if not directly controlled, by state-affiliated groups. While definitive attribution remains elusive, the mere possibility underscores how blurred the line between criminal botnets and state-controlled cyberweapons has become.

Another dimension is the use of botnets for information control. Large-scale DDoS campaigns can silence independent media outlets, flood online platforms with propaganda, or disrupt communication channels during protests. In 2019, during the Hong Kong protests, activists reported coordinated online disruptions that some experts attributed to botnet activity, although conclusive evidence was lacking. Whether directly state-driven or outsourced to criminal groups, the effect was the same: IoT botnets had become tools of political influence.

Looking ahead, the most concerning development is the potential fusion of IoT botnets with artificial intelligence. Traditional botnets rely on central commands or pre-programmed instructions. An AI-driven botnet, however, could autonomously adapt its behavior, choosing optimal targets, evading defenses, and maximizing impact without direct human oversight. In such a scenario, IoT botnets would cease to be blunt instruments of disruption and instead become intelligent, adaptive weapons, capable not just of causing chaos, but of waging protracted digital campaigns.

IoT botnets are not a passing phase; they are a structural feature of the digital age. Mirai may have been the first to capture headlines, but it was merely the opening act in a much longer saga. Bashlite, Hajime, Mozi, and countless other variants have demonstrated how quickly these armies evolve, adapt, and diversify. The danger lies not just in their destructive potential but in their persistence. Each new generation of IoT devices, rushed to market with little regard for security, replenishes the pool of recruits. Each new application of connectivity, from smart homes to industrial automation expands the battlefield. Meanwhile, the underground economy ensures that even low-skill actors can rent botnets on demand, while nation-states quietly consider how best to harness these invisible armies for strategic advantage. The rise of IoT botnets represents a grim irony. Devices meant to simplify life, increase efficiency, and connect the world have instead become the foundation of global cyber arsenals. The "things" of the Internet of Things are no longer passive endpoints they are conscripts in an endless digital war, their power hijacked, their purpose corrupted. For individuals, this means their own devices may be unwitting participants in attacks on hospitals, banks, or governments. For corporations, it means perpetual exposure to disruption and espionage. For nations, it means living under the constant shadow of invisible armies waiting to be mobilized.

The IoT Armageddon, in this sense, is already underway. It is not a single catastrophic event but a continuous reality: billions of devices, endlessly recruited, endlessly weaponized, endlessly turned against the very systems they were built to serve.

Chapter Seven

Medical IoT on Life Support

Few sectors embody the promise and peril of the Internet of Things (IoT) more starkly than healthcare. In an age where sensors, implants, and connected monitors promise unprecedented control over chronic illnesses, the same connectivity has opened pathways for malicious interference. Unlike attacks on smart TVs or webcams, the stakes here are not convenience or privacy, they are human lives.

Take, for instance, the case of connected pacemakers. In 2017, the U.S. Food and Drug Administration (FDA) issued an extraordinary recall: nearly half a million implanted pacemakers were found to be vulnerable to hacking. Researchers demonstrated that these life-saving devices could be remotely accessed and reprogrammed, potentially allowing an attacker to drain the battery or even deliver fatal shocks to the heart. To address the risk, patients were required to visit clinics for software updates to their implanted devices, an unsettling reminder that their most intimate lifeline could be weaponized. Insulin pumps tell a similar story. Diabetic patients increasingly rely on "smart pumps" that can automatically monitor glucose levels and administer precise doses of insulin. In 2019, medical device maker Medtronic recalled several models after vulnerabilities were discovered that allowed remote tampering. An attacker, theoretically, could deliver a massive overdose of insulin, inducing a deadly hypoglycemic event. Though no attacks were publicly reported, the possibility alone exposed the chilling reality: vulnerabilities in medical IoT devices transform everyday treatments into vectors of potential assassination. What makes these vulnerabilities particularly dangerous is their invisibility. Patients cannot "patch" a pacemaker or review the source code of their insulin pump. They must trust the manufacturer and the healthcare system. Even when updates are possible, many devices lack over-the-air update mechanisms, requiring in-person visits an impractical solution for many. Worse, legacy devices remain in circulation for years, sometimes decades, long after manufacturers cease supporting them. The rush to innovate often exacerbates the problem. Startups eager to disrupt healthcare race to market with new sensors, wearables, and monitoring tools, but security rarely keeps pace. Hospital procurement departments, meanwhile, are under pressure to cut costs, meaning the cheapest connected device often wins out over the most secure. The result is a landscape filled with vulnerable lifelines, devices designed to sustain life but ill-prepared to defend against invisible digital threats.

Hospitals Under Siege

While individual patients face unique risks, the broader healthcare system is equally vulnerable. Hospitals have become prime targets for ransomware gangs and state-backed hackers, and IoT plays a central role in both enabling and amplifying these attacks.

The WannaCry ransomware outbreak of 2017 was a stark warning. Originating from stolen cyberweapons developed by the U.S. National Security Agency (NSA), WannaCry spread rapidly across unpatched systems worldwide. Among the hardest hit was the United Kingdom's National Health Service (NHS). Hospitals were forced to cancel surgeries, divert ambulances, and delay treatments as critical systems shut down. While WannaCry did not specifically target IoT devices, the incident demonstrated how vulnerable the interconnected fabric of modern healthcare had become. Many of the NHS's impacted systems were tied to medical IoT infrastructure MRI machines, diagnostic tools, and other connected devices running outdated operating systems.

Since WannaCry, the situation has grown worse. In the United States alone, dozens of hospital networks have fallen victim to ransomware, often leading to temporary closures of emergency rooms. In some cases, patient care was directly affected. In 2020, a ransomware attack on a German hospital forced doctors to reroute a critical-care patient to another facility, where she later died. Prosecutors investigated the incident as a possible case of negligent homicide; the first time a patient's death was directly linked to a cyberattack. IoT magnifies these risks. Modern hospitals rely on thousands of connected devices, from infusion pumps and ventilators to wireless monitoring systems and smart beds. Each device is a potential entry point for attackers. In 2018, security researchers at McAfee demonstrated how they could hack a widely used infusion pump to change medication dosages, bypassing safety alarms. In another case, cybersecurity firm CyberMDX revealed vulnerabilities in hospital imaging equipment that could allow attackers to manipulate scans, potentially altering diagnoses. The systemic fragility is compounded by operational realities. Many hospitals run on tight margins, with limited resources to invest in cybersecurity. IT departments are often understaffed, and patching medical devices is not as simple as updating laptops. Regulatory constraints mean devices cannot be modified without manufacturer approval, and even when patches exist, applying them may require taking equipment offline an unacceptable risk in 24/7 medical environments.

As a result, many hospitals operate with known vulnerabilities, effectively gambling that they will not be targeted. But ransomware gangs have shown little mercy. In 2021, the FBI and the Cybersecurity and Infrastructure Security Agency (CISA) warned of an "increased and imminent" cyber threat to U.S. hospitals, noting that criminal groups were specifically targeting healthcare with ransomware campaigns. The COVID-19 pandemic, far from deterring attackers, created new opportunities, as overloaded hospitals struggled to balance patient care with digital resilience.

In the battlefield of cyberwarfare, hospitals have become soft targets and the integration of IoT has only widened the attack surface.

The Ethics of Hacking Healthcare

Healthcare attacks strike a unique nerve because they highlight the moral abyss of modern cyber conflict. When a bank is hacked, money can be recovered. When a social media platform is breached, data can be restored. But when a ventilator is disabled or an insulin pump is reprogrammed, lives may be lost irreversibly. The ethics of hacking healthcare, therefore, occupy a darker and more contested terrain.

For nation-states, healthcare systems are both attractive and sensitive targets. Intelligence agencies may seek medical records to blackmail individuals or gather insights into foreign leaders' health conditions. Military planners may view attacks on hospitals as a way to destabilize adversaries during conflict. In 2020, for example, reports surfaced that North Korean hackers targeted companies developing COVID-19 vaccines, presumably to steal intellectual property and gain strategic advantage. While these were espionage operations rather than direct attacks on patients, they revealed how healthcare IoT infrastructure is increasingly intertwined with national security.

Criminal groups, meanwhile, often justify attacks on hospitals as "just business." In 2020, the ransomware gang Ryuk unleashed a wave of attacks on U.S. hospitals, crippling networks at the height of the pandemic. Even after public pleas to spare medical facilities, the attacks continued. Some gangs have tried to draw ethical lines, claiming they avoid healthcare targets, but in practice these assurances are unreliable. The lucrative nature of hospital ransomware payouts often trumps morality. At the same time, ethical hackers' security researchers committed to exposing vulnerabilities to face their own dilemmas. In 2011, Jay Radcliffe, a diabetic security researcher, demonstrated how he could remotely hack his own insulin pump. His presentation at a security conference was controversial: some praised him for raising awareness, while others worried the disclosure could inspire malicious actors. Similar debates erupted when researcher Barnaby Jack showcased attacks against pacemakers, leading some to question whether public demonstrations of medical IoT hacks put patients at risk.

Yet without these disclosures, vulnerabilities might never be addressed. The FDA has since taken a more proactive role, issuing guidelines for medical device cybersecurity and encouraging coordinated vulnerability disclosure. Still, regulation lags behind reality. With thousands of manufacturers and millions of devices in circulation, ensuring comprehensive security remains an elusive goal.

The future of medical IoT security will depend on aligning incentives. Manufacturers must be compelled, through regulation, liability, or market pressure, to prioritize security from the outset. Hospitals must treat cybersecurity as a core element of patient safety, not an afterthought. And governments must recognize that protecting healthcare from cyberattacks is not only a moral imperative but also a strategic necessity.

The metaphor of the body is apt when thinking about medical IoT. Just as the human body relies on a network of organs and systems to sustain life, the modern healthcare ecosystem depends on a vast array of interconnected devices. But just as pathogens exploit weaknesses in the body, hackers exploit vulnerabilities in these digital systems.

The risks are no longer hypothetical. Pacemaker recalls, insulin pump vulnerabilities, ransomware-linked deaths, and hospital shutdowns have already demonstrated the real-world consequences of insecure medical IoT. The promise of connected healthcare, more personalized treatment, real-time monitoring, and improved outcomes is undeniable. But without robust security, that promise collapses into peril.

Patients, often unaware of the risks, live with devices that could theoretically be turned against them. Hospitals, stretched thin, juggle the demands of patient care with the realities of digital defense. And regulators, caught between fostering innovation and ensuring safety, struggle to keep pace with the accelerating tide of technological change.

The future of healthcare will be connected. That much is certain. The question is whether it will also be secure. If not, the very technologies designed to heal may instead become instruments of harm. In the broader story of the IoT Armageddon, the battlefield of medical IoT is among the most intimate and consequential. It is not merely about data or disruption; it is about life itself.

Chapter Eight

Smart Cities Dumb Security

The twenty-first century has been called the century of urbanization. By 2050, more than two-thirds of the world's population is expected to live in cities. To meet the demands of swelling populations, governments and technology firms have embraced the idea of "smart cities." These urban environments promise to harness sensors, networks, and artificial intelligence to optimize traffic flows, reduce energy waste, cut crime, and deliver more responsive public services. The Internet of Things (IoT) is the connective tissue that makes these promises possible.

At their core, smart cities have vast data ecosystems. Every traffic light, surveillance camera, bus stop, water meter, and electricity substation becomes a node in a digital nervous system. Traffic congestion can be alleviated through adaptive stoplights, waste can be optimized through smart bins that alert sanitation crews, and emergency services can be dispatched with real-time precision. The rhetoric is seductive: more efficient, more sustainable, and more livable cities.

But beneath this optimism lies an uncomfortable truth. In their rush to deploy smart technology, cities have often prioritized efficiency and cost over resilience and security. Procurement decisions favor the cheapest bidder, not the most secure. Devices are deployed with weak or default passwords, unencrypted communications, and little oversight. The result is an urban environment stitched together with millions of connected devices, many of which are vulnerable to attack. Smart cities may be smarter than the cities of the past, but in the rush to connect, they may also be far more fragile. The promise of connected cities cannot be separated from the peril they introduce. Every additional IoT node represents a potential entry point for hackers. When those nodes are embedded into critical infrastructure traffic control, energy distribution, and water treatment, the consequences of compromise move from nuisance to catastrophe. The dream of the smart city is therefore shadowed by the nightmare of the dumb security underpinning it.

The Architecture of Vulnerability

To understand why smart cities are so vulnerable, we must first examine how they are built. Unlike traditional infrastructure projects that follow decades-old engineering principles, smart city deployments often resemble technology experiments scaled to urban proportions. The rush to innovate has created a patchwork of systems from different vendors, operating on different protocols, with varying security standards.

Consider a typical smart intersection. It might include traffic cameras from one manufacturer, signal controllers from another, pedestrian sensors from a third, and environmental monitoring equipment from a fourth. Each device connects to the network differently, some via Wi-Fi, others through cellular modems, still others using proprietary wireless protocols. This heterogeneity, while enabling rapid deployment and cost optimization, creates a security nightmare.

The problem is compounded by the sheer scale of deployment. A major city might install tens of thousands of IoT devices across its territory in a matter of months. Quality control becomes nearly impossible. Security audits that might be routine for a handful of critical systems become logistically overwhelming when applied to thousands of distributed sensors. The result is an urban environment where security is inversely proportional to convenience.

Legacy systems add another layer of complexity. Cities cannot simply rip out decades of existing infrastructure and start fresh. Instead, they must integrate smart technologies with aging systems that were never designed for network connectivity. A water treatment plant built in the 1970s might receive digital sensors and remote monitoring capabilities, but its fundamental control systems remain rooted in pre-internet engineering. These hybrid environments create security blind spots where old and new systems interact in unpredictable ways.

Cracks in the Digital Pavement

The vulnerabilities of smart cities are not hypothetical. Across the globe, incidents have already revealed the cracks in their digital foundations.

In 2006, long before the smart city concept became mainstream, a group of disgruntled engineers in Los Angeles successfully hacked the city's traffic signal system during a labor dispute. They caused days of gridlock by manually overriding light sequences. That incident occurred with a relatively closed system. Today, with internet-connected traffic infrastructure proliferating, the attack surface is exponentially larger. In 2014, researchers in Michigan demonstrated how they could wirelessly hack connected traffic lights, changing signals at will. The vulnerabilities stemmed from unencrypted wireless communications and default passwords, simple flaws with dangerous consequences.

The Michigan researchers' work revealed troubling patterns that extend far beyond traffic systems. They found that many smart city devices use standard, well-known default passwords that are never changed during installation.

Communication protocols often lack basic encryption, transmitting commands and data in plain text that can be easily intercepted. Perhaps most concerning, many systems lack proper authentication mechanisms, meaning that any device that can connect to the network is trusted by default.

Surveillance systems are another common weak point. In 2017, hackers compromised more than 120 police surveillance cameras across Washington, D.C., just days before the presidential inauguration. The breach prevented the cameras from recording, forcing a citywide scramble to restore functionality in time for the event. Though the attack was resolved, it showcased how critical public safety infrastructure could be temporarily blinded by a determined adversary.

The Washington D.C. incident highlighted a particular vulnerability in smart city surveillance networks: their centralized management systems. While individual cameras might be distributed across a city, they often connect to centralized servers for storage and analysis. Compromising these central systems can effectively disable surveillance across entire districts. This architectural choice, made for efficiency and cost savings, creates single points of failure that amplify the impact of successful attacks.

Water systems, too, have been targeted. In 2021, hackers gained remote access to the water treatment plant of Oldsmar, Florida. They attempted to increase the level of sodium hydroxide essentially lye in the water supply to poisonous levels. Luckily, the manipulation was quickly noticed by an operator, and no harm occurred. But the incident made clear that insecure IoT systems in critical utilities could turn essential services into weapons. The Oldsmar attack was particularly revealing because it demonstrated how remote access systems, installed to improve operational efficiency, could become attack vectors. The hackers gained access through a remote desktop application that lacked multi-factor authentication. Once inside the network, they found that critical control systems were accessible from the same network segment, with no additional security barriers. This "flat" network architecture, while simpler to manage, eliminates the defense-in-depth principles that cybersecurity professionals consider essential.

Even seemingly minor systems can create outsized disruptions. Smart streetlights, parking meters, and waste bins, if hijacked, could cause chaos in unexpected ways. Imagine a coordinated attack disabling traffic sensors during rush hour, plunging downtown cores into paralyzed congestion. Or consider how compromised environmental sensors could report false air quality readings, influencing public behavior or policy decisions. Smart parking systems present a particularly interesting case study. These networks of sensors, designed to help drivers find available spaces, typically communicate location and occupancy data to central servers. However, researchers have demonstrated that these systems can be manipulated to create artificial scarcity, directing traffic to specific areas or creating congestion as a form of economic warfare. The psychological impact of such attacks turning routine urban navigation into a source of frustration and unpredictability illustrates how smart city vulnerabilities extend beyond purely technical consequences.

The Human Factor

While technical vulnerabilities dominate headlines, the human element often proves to be the weakest link in smart city security. The complexity of these systems means that even well-intentioned operators can inadvertently create security gaps.

Municipal IT departments, often understaffed and underfunded, struggle to keep pace with the security requirements of rapidly expanding IoT networks. Unlike traditional IT environments where security teams focus on a limited number of servers and workstations, smart cities require monitoring thousands of diverse devices spread across vast geographical areas. The skillset required to secure a traffic management system differs significantly from that needed to protect water treatment facilities, yet cities often expect small teams to handle both.

Training presents another challenge. As cities deploy new smart technologies, they must simultaneously train operators, maintenance staff, and security personnel on unfamiliar systems. In the rush to get services online, security training often takes a backseat to operational training. Employees learn how to use new systems but not necessarily how to use them securely. This knowledge gap can persist for years, as busy municipal workers focus on day-to-day operations rather than security best practices. The vendor ecosystem adds complexity to the human factor. Smart city deployments typically involve multiple contractors and subcontractors, each with their own security practices and personnel. Coordinating security standards across this fragmented ecosystem proves challenging. A city might implement strong security policies for its core systems, only to discover that a subcontractor installing parking sensors has been using default passwords and unencrypted communications. Procurement processes, designed for traditional infrastructure projects, often fail to adequately evaluate cybersecurity capabilities. Purchasing departments accustomed to buying concrete and steel struggle to assess the relative security merits of competing IoT solutions. Technical specifications might include security requirements, but evaluating vendor compliance requires expertise that many municipal buyers lack. The result is a procurement process that inadvertently rewards vendors who promise comprehensive security but may not deliver it in practice.

Cascading Failures and System Dependencies

The interconnected nature of smart cities means that a security breach in one system can trigger failures across multiple domains. These cascading failures represent one of the most dangerous aspects of urban IoT vulnerabilities.

Consider how a cyberattack on traffic management systems could ripple through a city. Initially, the attack might cause congestion by disrupting signal timing. This congestion could delay emergency response vehicles, potentially costing lives in medical emergencies. Simultaneously, delivery trucks carrying fuel to gas stations might be stuck in traffic, leading to fuel shortages that affect backup power generators at hospitals and data centers. As these generators fail, communication systems begin to degrade, hampering the city's ability to coordinate its response to the original cyber incident.

This scenario illustrates how smart cities, optimized for efficiency, can become brittle under stress. The same interconnections that enable optimization in normal conditions can accelerate the spread of failures during crisis. Traditional cities, with their redundant and often inefficient systems, might be less optimal but prove more resilient when components fail.

Smart grid systems present particularly complex dependency challenges. Modern electrical grids increasingly rely on IoT sensors and automated controls to balance supply and demand in real-time. These systems can react to changing conditions within seconds, automatically routing power around failed components or adjusting generation to match consumption patterns. However, this automation depends on the integrity of sensor data and control communications. Corrupted data or compromised control channels can cause the smart grid to make decisions that destabilize rather than optimize the electrical system.

The integration of renewable energy sources adds another layer of complexity. Solar panels and wind turbines, connected through smart inverters and monitoring systems, contribute variable amounts of power to the grid. Managing this variability requires sophisticated forecasting and control systems that depend heavily on IoT data. An attack that corrupts weather sensors or manipulates renewable energy forecasts could force grid operators to make poor decisions about backup power generation, potentially leading to blackouts or equipment damage.

The Economics of Insecurity

Understanding why smart cities remain vulnerable requires examining the economic incentives that drive their development. The current market structure often rewards rapid deployment and low costs over security and resilience.

Vendors competing for smart city contracts face intense pressure to minimize upfront costs. Security features, which add complexity and expense, become easy targets for cost-cutting. A vendor might offer a traffic management system at a significantly lower price than competitors by using cheaper, less secure communication modules or by skipping security testing during development. Municipal buyers, operating under tight budget constraints, may choose the lower-cost option without fully understanding the long-term security implications. The separation between procurement and operations within city governments exacerbates this problem. The department that buys smart city technology may not be the same department that operates and maintains it. Procurement officials, focused on staying within budget and meeting deployment timelines, may not fully appreciate the ongoing costs and risks associated with insecure systems. Operations staff, who must live with these decisions for years or decades, often have little input into the initial purchasing process.

Liability structures further distort incentives. When smart city systems fail or are compromised, the costs are typically borne by the city and its residents rather than the technology vendors. Vendors may offer warranties that cover hardware replacement but not the broader economic and social costs of system failures. This externalization of risk removes a key market incentive for vendors to invest in robust security measures. The rapid pace of technological change also works against security. Smart city vendors, eager to stay competitive, frequently release new products and features without comprehensive security testing. The pressure to be first to market with new capabilities can override security concerns. Cities, meanwhile, fear being left behind and may rush to adopt new technologies without adequate evaluation of their security implications.

Weaponizing Urban IoT

If hackers can already blind cameras, hijack traffic lights, and tamper with water supplies, what happens when these capabilities are scaled, weaponized, and deployed in geopolitical conflict? The implications are sobering. Imagine a city under cyber siege. At the onset of hostilities, its traffic lights are thrown into chaos, creating gridlock that paralyzes emergency response. Surveillance cameras suddenly go dark, leaving law enforcement blind. Power distribution nodes begin to fail, plunging neighborhoods into rolling blackouts. Simultaneously, water treatment plants receive false commands, forcing operators to shut down systems to avoid contamination. Each individual disruption might be manageable in isolation. Together, they represent cascading failures capable of grinding a city to a halt. This scenario is not pure speculation. In Ukraine, cyberattacks have repeatedly targeted critical infrastructure since 2015. Hackers have taken down power grids in Kyiv during the dead of winter, leaving hundreds of thousands without electricity. While those attacks were not specifically IoT-driven, the integration of IoT into critical systems only increases the potential for disruption. In a future conflict, smart cities could become digital battlegrounds where urban life itself is the casualty.

The psychological dimension of smart city attacks deserves particular attention. Unlike traditional military targets, smart city infrastructure is intimately connected to civilian daily life. An attack that disrupts traffic, water, and power doesn't just degrade military capabilities, it directly impacts every resident's quality of life. This creates opportunities for adversaries to apply pressure on civilian populations, potentially influencing political decisions or undermining social cohesion.

Nation-states have already demonstrated sophisticated cyber capabilities against urban infrastructure. The Stuxnet attack on Iranian nuclear facilities showed how malware could manipulate industrial control systems with surgical precision. Similar techniques could be applied to smart city systems, causing failures that appear accidentally while actually being carefully orchestrated. A traffic signal that malfunctions at precisely the wrong moment, or a water treatment plant that develops "random" faults during a crisis, could be signs of invisible cyber warfare. The interdependence of smart city systems compounds the risk. Traffic management relies on power, which relies on communications, which relies on sensors, all of which may share overlapping vulnerabilities. A compromise in one sector can cascade into others. An attack that disables traffic lights could impede fuel deliveries, which then disrupts emergency generator supply, which further cripples' hospitals already straining under cyber assault. Smart cities, designed for efficiency, risk becoming brittle in crisis.

Nation-states understand these dynamics. Urban IoT represents both a tempting espionage target and a potential offensive weapon. Intelligence agencies may seek to quietly infiltrate smart city systems, planting back doors that can be activated during conflict. Criminal groups, meanwhile, may exploit vulnerabilities for ransom, threatening to plunge cities into chaos unless paid. The convergence of nation-state and criminal motives creates a volatile environment where the line between cyberwarfare and cybercrime blurs.

Looking ahead, the weaponization of urban IoT may evolve further with the integration of artificial intelligence. Autonomous botnets could coordinate citywide disruptions with precision timing, maximizing chaos while evading detection. Attackers could leverage machine learning to identify weak points in real-time, escalating the attack dynamically. Unlike traditional warfare, such campaigns could unfold without a single shot fired, yet their impact could rival physical bombardment.

Emerging Threats and Future Vulnerabilities

As smart cities continue to evolve, new categories of vulnerabilities are emerging that go beyond traditional cybersecurity concerns. The integration of artificial intelligence, the deployment of 5G networks and the increasing use of cloud services are creating new attack surfaces that cities are only beginning to understand.

AI systems used in smart cities, while powerful, introduce unique vulnerabilities. Machine learning models can be fooled by adversarial inputs carefully crafted data designed to cause AI systems to make incorrect decisions. An attacker might manipulate traffic sensors to feed false data to AI traffic management systems, causing them to create congestion rather than alleviate it. Similarly, AI-powered surveillance systems could be fooled by carefully designed patterns or objects that cause them to miss genuine security threats while flagging innocent behavior.

The deployment of 5G networks promises to accelerate smart city development by providing high-speed, low-latency connectivity for IoT devices. However, 5G also introduces new security challenges. The increased network capacity enables more devices to connect simultaneously, expanding the attack surface exponentially. The lower latency enables real-time control applications but also means that successful attacks can have immediate physical consequences. Edge computing, deployed to support 5G applications, distributes computing power throughout the city but also distributes potential attack targets.

Cloud services, increasingly used to manage smart city data and applications, create new categories of risk. While cloud providers typically offer strong security capabilities, the complexity of cloud configurations can lead to vulnerabilities. Misconfigured cloud storage systems have already exposed sensitive government data in numerous incidents. As cities move more of their smart infrastructure to cloud platforms, similar misconfigurations could expose critical operational data or provide attackers with entry points into urban systems.

Conclusion: Cities at the Crossroads

Smart cities embody both the best and worst of the IoT revolution. They offer the promise of cleaner air, reduced congestion, safer streets, and more sustainable living. But they also expose entire populations to risks that are difficult to comprehend and harder to mitigate. The cracks in the digital pavement are already visible: hacked traffic systems, hijacked surveillance cameras, and poisoned water treatment plants. These are not isolated anomalies, they are warning shots. As more cities embrace the smart paradigm, the attack surface expands exponentially. Without a fundamental shift in priorities, urban IoT risks becoming a weapon against the very populations it was meant to serve.

The path forward requires treating cybersecurity as a core component of urban planning, not an afterthought. Procurement processes must reward security as much as cost and efficiency. Standards must enforce encryption, authentication, and regular patching. Public-private partnerships must ensure that vendors bear responsibility for the resilience of their products. And perhaps most importantly, cities must invest in the human expertise needed to secure complex, interconnected systems.

This investment extends beyond hiring cybersecurity professionals. Cities need to develop organizational cultures that prioritize security alongside efficiency. They need procurement processes that can effectively evaluate cybersecurity capabilities. They need incident response capabilities that can handle city-scale emergencies. And they need governance structures that can coordinate security across the diverse systems and stakeholders that comprise a modern smart city.

The technical challenges are significant, but they are solvable. Encryption technologies exist to protect communications. Authentication systems can verify device identities. Network segmentation can contain the spread of attacks. Monitoring systems can detect unusual behavior. The question is not whether cities can be made more secure, but whether they will commit the resources and attention needed to implement these solutions. Perhaps most importantly, citizens must recognize that convenience is not free; it is paid for in exposure to risk. The smart city vision of frictionless urban living depends on unprecedented levels of data collection and system integration. Citizens must decide what level of risk they are willing to accept in exchange for the promised benefits of smart city technology.

Cities are at a crossroads. They can continue to chase efficiency, layering connectivity upon connectivity until urban life becomes a house of cards. Or they can confront the vulnerabilities head-on, building resilience into the digital foundations of tomorrow's metropolises. The choice is not abstract. The next blackout, gridlock, or water crisis may not come from natural disaster or human error but from invisible hands manipulating the digital strings of the smart city. If the Internet of Things is the nervous system of modern life, then cities are its beating heart. And the security of that heart may determine the survival of the body politic in the decades to come.

Chapter Nine

When Cars Become Weapons

For most of the twentieth century, cars were mechanical machines. Steel, combustion, hydraulics, and little else. A mechanic with a wrench and grease under his fingernails could diagnose and repair almost anything. But by the early twenty-first century, the automobile began its metamorphosis into something far more complex: a computer on wheels.

Today, the modern car is a rolling data center. Dozens of sensors monitor tire pressure, engine function, and driver behavior. Telematics units connect vehicles to the cloud, streaming diagnostics to manufacturers and insurers. Infotainment systems integrate seamlessly with smartphones. Navigation, entertainment, climate, and even seat adjustments are increasingly software-driven. For electric vehicles, software is the beating heart, governing not just entertainment but propulsion, braking, and charging.

Over-the-air (OTA) updates, a feature pioneered by Tesla, mean that vehicles are no longer static products but dynamic platforms, patched and upgraded remotely. In theory, this allows automakers to improve performance, extend range, and patch vulnerabilities without costly recalls. In practice, it means that cars now live permanently online. Each connection is a potential doorway. Autonomous vehicles push this logic further still. Self-driving systems depend on real-time sensor fusion, communication with other vehicles, and constant updates. The dream of safer roads free of human error, fatigue, or distraction is predicated on a vehicle's ability to trust its own digital systems. But what if that trust is misplaced? When every car is part of a network, every vulnerability becomes contagious.

The connected car revolution promises efficiency and convenience. But by making vehicles smarter, we have also made them hackable. The stakes are uniquely high: a compromised smartphone can drain your bank account, but a compromised car can take your life.

Hacked at 70 Miles Per Hour

The fragility of connected cars was brought into sharp focus in July 2015. That summer, security researchers Charlie Miller and Chris Valasek remotely hacked a Jeep Cherokee as it barreled down a highway at 70 miles per hour. From miles away, they manipulated the air conditioning, the windshield wipers, and the stereo and then escalated to disabling the transmission altogether. The driver, a journalist covering the story, suddenly found himself powerless as his vehicle coasted on a busy interstate.

The demonstration was not malicious; it was staged to raise awareness. But the implications were chilling. Fiat Chrysler was forced to recall 1.4 million vehicles to patch the vulnerability. It was the first time the public truly understood that a car could be hacked like a computer. The Jeep case was dramatic, but not isolated. Tesla vehicles, with their deep reliance on software, have been frequent targets of white-hat researchers. In 2016, a Chinese hacking group known as Keen Security Lab remotely took control of a Tesla Model S, opening doors, manipulating the dashboard, and engaging the brakes at low speed. Tesla responded quickly with patches, but the incident underscored how even the most technologically advanced automakers are not immune.

BMW has faced similar scrutiny. In 2015, the German auto giant admitted that 2.2 million of its connected cars were vulnerable to remote hacks through the ConnectedDrive system. Researchers demonstrated how insecure communications could allow attackers to remotely unlock doors, exposing owners to theft. Beyond high-profile brands, vulnerabilities abound in less glamorous domains. Bluetooth exploits allow hackers to pair with infotainment systems and pivot into deeper vehicle controls. Telematics units widely used in fleet management are often shipped with default credentials and weak authentication, making them ripe for exploitation. Even simple key-fob systems have proven fallible, with relay attacks allowing thieves to unlock and drive away modern cars in seconds.

The line between annoyance and existential risk is blurry. A hacker who unlocks your doors may steal your belongings. A hacker who disables your brakes may steal your life. The Jeep hack made headlines because it proved the latter scenario is technically feasible. And as vehicles become more connected, the attack surface only grows.

From Getaway Cars to Cyberweapons

If cars can be hacked, then cars can be weaponized. What was once the domain of car thieves could become the playground of terrorists, criminals, and nation-states.

Consider a coordinated attack in a major city. Hackers compromise hundreds of vehicles simultaneously, disabling their brakes or steering at rush hour. The result is not just traffic congestion but mass casualties, with pileups stretching for miles. Emergency services would be overwhelmed, and panic could spread as drivers realize they no longer control their cars. The ability to remotely weaponize fleets of vehicles transforms ordinary urban environments into potential war zones. Terrorists could exploit vulnerabilities for targeted assassinations. If a political leader's car is connected, an attacker may not need explosives, they could simply hijack the vehicle's controls at a critical moment. Criminal groups could deploy ransomware, locking drivers out of their cars until a payment is made. Unlike digital-only ransoms, these would directly immobilize victims in their daily lives, creating immediate pressure to comply.

The risks extend beyond consumer vehicles. Logistics fleets are the lifeblood of modern economies. Connected trucks deliver food, medicine, and fuel. A large-scale hack of fleet telematics could grind supply chains to a halt, triggering economic paralysis. In 2018, researchers demonstrated vulnerabilities in commercial truck systems that allowed remote manipulation of braking and acceleration. While no catastrophic event has yet occurred, the feasibility is proven.

Military transport presents another dimension. Armored vehicles, supply convoys, and even drones increasingly depend on IoT integration for navigation and communication. A compromised logistics chain in wartime could prove devastating. The line between civilian and military risk blurs as both rely on the same suppliers, technologies, and networks. Looking further ahead, the specter of vehicular botnets looms large. Just as malware like Mirai conscripted IoT cameras into massive denial-of-service attacks, future malware could enslave fleets of vehicles. An AI-driven "car swarm" could be weaponized, instructing thousands of vehicles to accelerate simultaneously, block highways, or ram infrastructure. The physics of several tons of steel in motion make this more destructive than any server farm takedown. It is not hyperbole to suggest that cars may become the Stuxnet of the streets. Just as Stuxnet demonstrated that malware could cause physical destruction to nuclear centrifuges, vehicular botnets could turn everyday transportation into a weapon of mass disruption.

The automobile has always been a symbol of freedom. The open road represents autonomy, mobility, and control. Yet in the age of IoT, that control is increasingly illusory. Drivers may grip the steering wheel, but unseen lines of code, wireless updates, and cloud connections hold ultimate authority. The connected car revolution is irreversible. Consumers demand integration with their digital lives, regulators push for safety enhancements like collision avoidance, and automakers compete to differentiate through software. But every advance deepens dependence on systems that remain insecure.

What is needed is a fundamental shift in how vehicles are designed, tested, and secure. Cybersecurity must be treated not as a bolt-on feature but as a core component of automotive safety. Just as seatbelts and airbags became mandatory after years of preventable deaths, secure coding practices, encrypted communications, and rigorous penetration testing must become standard. Manufacturers must commit to long-term software support, ensuring that cars remain patched for their full lifecycle not just until the next model year.

The road ahead is perilous. The same vehicles that promise to chauffeur us into a safer, smarter future may also become instruments of chaos if left undefended. Cars, once mere machines, are now nodes in a vast digital network. And in a world where everything connected can be hacked, the freedom of the open road could one day be weaponized against us all.

Chapter Ten

Securing the Internet of Everything

The Internet of Things is not a niche technology. It is not a trend. It is not something we can opt into or out of as individuals. It is the invisible scaffolding of modern life: homes, cities, hospitals, cars, industries, militaries, even our own bodies. And with each passing year, the scaffolding grows denser. Analysts project that by the mid-2030s, we may live in a world with hundreds of billions of connected devices. Some estimates already place the number above 25 billion today.

Every one of those connections is a potential point of entry for an attacker. Every smart thermostat, every connected security camera, every Wi-Fi-enabled heart monitor, and every industrial control sensor is both a tool of progress and a possible liability. The attack surface has grown beyond comprehension. Unlike traditional computing devices, IoT is not centrally managed. A single network may contain dozens of vendors, protocols, and software stacks, each with their own vulnerabilities.

The scale alone changes the game. In the 1990s, cybersecurity was about protecting computers. In the 2000s, it was about protecting networks. In the 2010s, it was about protecting cloud infrastructures and mobile ecosystems. Now, in the 2020s and beyond, it is about protecting everything on the Internet of Everything. This is not merely a technical challenge. It is a societal one.

Reactive patching of the model that has defined cybersecurity for decades will never be enough in this landscape. When a new vulnerability is discovered in a web browser, a patch can be pushed overnight. But when a flaw is found in a pacemaker, a connected MRI machine, or a factory robot, patching is often impossible or takes months. In many cases, devices are deployed and forgotten, left vulnerable for years until they become weapons in botnets like Mirai, Mozi, or Hajime. The truth is sobering **we cannot secure the IoT world by accident or improvisation.** It requires deliberate architecture, a shift in priorities, and the courage to put safety above speed, resilience above convenience.

Principles for Defending the Undefendable

Securing the Internet of Everything will not be achieved through a single innovation or breakthrough. Instead, it requires a philosophical shift across governments, industries, and individuals.

1. Security by Design, Not Neglect For decades, consumer technology has operated on a reckless cycle: ship it fast, patch it later. IoT magnifies the risks of this approach. A webcam with default passwords can be hijacked into a global botnet within hours of being plugged in. A connected door lock with a sloppy firmware update mechanism could be exploited to trap families inside their homes.

Security must be **baked in from the start**, not bolted on as an afterthought. This means manufacturers committing to:

- Encrypted communications as a baseline.
- Strong authentication mechanisms.
- Secure boot processes to prevent malicious firmware.
- Long-term software support commitments.

Just as seatbelts became non-negotiable in cars, cybersecurity must become non-negotiable in connected devices.

2. Regulation and Accountability Left to their own devices; most manufacturers will prioritize cost and speed to market over security. That is not cynicism; it is economics. A $30 smart camera cannot include five years of patch support unless governments mandate it or consumers demand it.

We are beginning to see progress. The European Union's Cyber Resilience Act seeks to impose minimum security requirements on connected devices. The U.S. has introduced labeling systems to help consumers identify secure IoT products. Japan has pushed ISPs to scan networks for devices with weak passwords and notify owners.

But these efforts are fragmented. What is needed is a global baseline, a Geneva Convention for IoT. Just as international aviation standards ensure safety across borders, global cybersecurity standards could ensure that a device manufactured in Shenzhen, sold in Nairobi, and deployed in São Paulo meets minimum requirements.

3. Shared Responsibility Manufacturers cannot carry the burden alone. Governments must enforce standards, and users must recognize that convenience without security is a false economy. Hospitals must demand rigorous security audits before deploying medical IoT. Cities must weigh the risks of embedding thousands of unsecured sensors in their streets. Businesses must budget for long-term device maintenance, not just initial deployment.

In an interconnected world, security is not a private good; it is a public one. A single unsecured camera can be part of an attack that takes down global services. Responsibility must be distributed across all stakeholders.

Building Resilience for the Next Era

Even with best practices and regulation, perfection is impossible. Vulnerabilities will continue to emerge. Attackers will continue to innovate. What matters is building systems that bend without breaking, that can absorb attacks without cascading into catastrophe.

Layered Defense IoT security must be treated as an ecosystem challenge. Devices should not be trusted blindly just because they are inside a network. Zero-trust architectures where every connection is authenticated and verified must extend into IoT. Network segmentation can prevent a single compromised camera from reaching critical hospital equipment. Monitoring systems must detect anomalous behavior like a thermostat suddenly generating gigabytes of outbound traffic and shut it down automatically.

AI-Driven Defense The scale of IoT makes human monitoring impossible. Artificial intelligence will be essential for detecting and responding to threats in real time. Already, AI systems are being trained to spot abnormal device behavior, identify botnet recruitment patterns, and isolate compromised nodes. But AI is not a silver bullet. Attackers will use it too, generating polymorphic malware and adaptive attacks. The defense race will become increasingly autonomous, machine versus machine.

Ethical Hacking and Responsible Disclosure White-hat hackers like those who exposed the Jeep Cherokee and Tesla vulnerabilities, are critical allies. Their work forces manufacturers to confront uncomfortable truths before criminals exploit them. Governments and corporations must expand bug bounty programs, protect ethical researchers from legal retaliation, and foster a culture where finding vulnerabilities is celebrated, not punished.

Cyber Diplomacy The weaponization of IoT is not just a criminal threat; it is a geopolitical one. Nation-states are already probing each other's infrastructure, planting digital landmines for future conflicts. A cyberattack on a smart grid or hospital system could be as devastating as a missile strike. The world urgently needs cyber diplomacy agreements that limit attacks on civilian IoT, akin to conventions that prohibit chemical weapons. While enforcement will be difficult, norms must start somewhere.

The Internet of Everything is here. We cannot roll it back. We cannot uninvent connected cars, smart cities, or medical IoT. We can only choose whether to build them securely or let them evolve into weapons of our own destruction. The dark road is easy to imagine botnets of millions of devices launching attacks that cripple economies, hacked fleets turned into car bombs, hospitals paralyzed mid-surgery by ransomware, and cities brought to their knees by hijacked traffic lights and power grids. The seeds of this future already exist. Mirai, Mozi, Hajime, and Bashlite these were warning shots, not final blows.

And yet, there is another road. A future where manufacturers embrace security by design. Where regulators enforce global standards. Where hospitals, cities, and industries treat cybersecurity as essential infrastructure. Where AI systems act as digital immune systems, spotting infections before they spread. Where ethical hackers are allies, not adversaries. We stand at the threshold between catastrophe and control. The IoT Armageddon is not inevitable. It is a choice. If we act with foresight, discipline, and courage, we can secure the Internet of Everything. If we do not, then the very devices meant to empower us will become the tools of our undoing.

www.ingramcontent.com/pod-product-compliance
Lightning Source LLC
Chambersburg PA
CBHW021215250926
51852CB00006B/15
* 9 7 8 8 8 3 9 8 1 7 7 5 4 *